DEATH
IN THE
DARK
CONTINENT

By the same author
DEATH IN THE LONG GRASS
DEATH IN THE SILENT PLACES

DEATH
IN THE
DARK
CONTINENT

Peter Hathaway Capstick

St. Martin's Press
New York

Grateful acknowledgment is made to M. Philip Kahl for permission to reprint the photos on pages x, 1, 15, 95, 145, and 191; and to Bob D'Olivo for the photo on page 67.

Design by Kingsley Parker

Library of Congress Cataloging in Publication Data

Capstick, Peter Hathaway.
    Death in the Dark Continent.

    1. Big game hunting—Africa. I. Title.
SK251.C268 1983   799'.2'6'0967   83-3111
ISBN 0-312-18615-0

20 19 18 17 16 15 14 13 12 11

With love to my mother,
Ruth Hathaway Connor Capstick,
who made it all possible.

CONTENTS

Acknowledgments   ix

Foreword   xi

1 The Big Five   1

2 Buffalo   15

3 Rhino   67

4 Elephant   95

5 Leopard   145

6 Lion   191

ACKNOWLEDGMENTS

The author would like to express his thanks and appreciation to the following for their trouble and help in the creation of this book:

Jessica Grace Coughlan, of Pietermaritzburg, South Africa, for providing such excellent and useful research.

Thomas J. Siatos, Vice President and Executive Publisher of, among others, Petersen's *Hunting* and *Guns & Ammo* magazines for permission to use the photo of his taking a bull rhino.

Bob D'Olivo, the intrepid Petersen photographer who took the picture of Tom Siatos, with his usual talent.

Les Pockell of St. Martin's Press, Inc., for his perception and direction.

Mrs. Doyle Williams Smelko for her fine work in the preparation of the manuscript.

Dr. M. Philip Kahl, old friend and *compadre,* who made available most of the photographs used in this book.

Mr. Bruce McIvor, for permission to include his nearly fatal brush with a Cape buffalo.

FOREWORD

If you doubt that man is by nature a predator, this book will inspire little in you but perhaps rage. It is not for you, to whom the challenge of hunting dangerous game seems some throwback to our primeval, perhaps even bestial, ways, ways to be apologized for in light of our recently self-bestowed nobility. If you disbelieve that man has a collective genetic memory of the old skills that helped change him from savage to space traveler, this is not your book.

Twenty million Americans believe otherwise and prove it by purchasing one or another form of hunting license each year. Added to these millions are of course untold hundreds of thousands more who don't actually hunt but still conduct an affair of the heart and mind with the weapons and mystique of the chase: handgun shooters, claybird shooters, and archers; and precision match riflemen in even more millions. More than two million alone pay dues to the National Rifle Association, the great nemesis of those who would run others' lives for them.

Either an apology for the morality of hunting under the sportsman's ethic or a defense of the hunter as the best friend of wildlife might seem appropriate for a more philosophic work. The facts are the facts. Should your interest be more than emotionally based, any appropriate government agency will be happy to supply exact information that clearly demonstrates the increase of game through direct funding by hunting-related taxes and licenses. And not just in America. Tremendous areas not overrun by Marxist regimes (who generally consider sport hunting decadent, a leftover pastime of the idle rich), such as South Africa, have many times the number of big game animals they had even decades ago. The reason? Land will rise to its highest and best use. In much of Africa, this means safari hunting under carefully controlled circumstances, for it not only provides excellent game management for the hunted species but also economic justification for the maintenance of wild habitat that would otherwise become farm or range land. This benefits all forms of wildlife, including man and his progeny. Once the wilds are gone, they're gone forever.

If on the other hand you prefer the sorcery of a flickering campfire on a chill evening to the late movie; if a far-off gabble of geese against a full moon orchestrating the waft of venison sizzling in butter is preferable to the best Maxim's has to offer; if you would rather be chilled, wet, and excited than warm, dry, and bored, this just might appeal to you. I hope you enjoy it.

Peter Hathaway Capstick
Pretoria, South Africa
November 1982

"To my deep mortification my father once said to me, 'You care for nothing but shooting, dogs and rat-catching, and you will be a disgrace to yourself and all your family.'"

—*Charles Darwin*

1 THE BIG FIVE

SINCE THE 1960s, when I first became a professional hunter in what finally tallied up to be three African nations, I have not been on a single safari on which, when the campfire embers turned the color of the reflected blood red of crocodiles' eyes, the conversation did not drift to what may be hunting's oldest question: What is the most dangerous game?

Funny you'd ask. . . .

Sorting out the relative deadliness of the African plug-uglies who will happily include you on their dance cards if you step on their toes is rather like determining the comparative merits of blond, brunette, and redheaded ladies. All are potentially deadly, but some a bit more than others, depending upon local conditions.

It would seem to me appropriate, before getting in waist deep, to recognize that really dangerous game is by no means limited to Africa or Las Vegas. Asia still has the ubiquitous leopards, by all reports in pretty fair numbers. Not so the tiger, yet Sahib Stripes still eats a couple of hundred potential U.N. delegates every year despite his endangered status. There's also that great wild bison, the gaur, as well as a very few pockets of seledang, banteng, and other crossword puzzle candidates in a rapidly dwindling wilderness that used to be the land of the *pukka* sahib.

As a tropical bird, nothing gives me a more smug feeling than to tell you that the closest I ever knowingly came to a wild polar bear was in 1964 in Goose Bay, Labrador, at minus fifty-five degrees Fahrenheit. As far as I recall, except for the bear's leaving some very large pawprints in a hell of a lot of snow, we mutually agreed to call it off. Further, I attempted to donate my lifetime potential of grizzlies and jaguars to the Smithsonian some years ago about the same time that Harvard turned down my body. Apparently there are a lot of bright people at both institutions.

Alas, Africa has not treated me with such consideration. I know scads more than I would have liked about lions, leopards, and rhinos, and if a vote were taken among elephants or buffalo I would probably be listed by acclamation as "the one who got away." Actually, I'm a very odd sort to have become a paid *bwana,* having a considerably greater regard for my anatomic nether regions than for even substantial lucre, itself rare enough in the safari business. Anyhow, by today's standards I have had a reasonable amount of experience with Africa's dangerous game under modern conditions, the relative time frame of my own shenanigans and those of earlier hunters being highly germane to determining the Big Five of dangerous game and which among them is the most accomplished felon, even if provoked.

Since I first started hunting and shooting, back at the age of eight, any money I had left over from buying my weekly stipend of .22 short cartridges went into books on hunting, Africa, and every now and then a few slightly racier subjects. That was a bit less than a century ago, or so it seems. But at least I was able to accumulate a pretty decent library of the works of guys who had *really* done the stuff when it was still there to do. Cumming and Harris track along my bookshelves, overlapping spoors with Baker, Bell, Rainsford, Tjader, Blixen, Foran, Hunter, Stigand, Ionides, Lyell, Roosevelt, and a regiment of equal luminaries to whom life's greatest reward was the privilege of testing their nerve, strength, skill, and honor against the world's most dangerous game. Many paid the bill with their lives in half-forgotten places like the Lado Enclave and the Tana Valley, the Luangwa and the Omo, the Ruwenzoris and the Cashans. Some hunted unabashedly for economic reasons, mainly that most magnificent company of extraordinary individualists since the American mountain men or the few wandering samurai sword masters, the professional ivory hunters. But more of this breed later. Others were private souls who devoted their lives to hunting almost as much for the sheer experience the bush afforded than for any other factor. Frederick C. Selous, the great naturalist and hunter killed by a German bullet in 1917 in today's Tanzania, typified this breed. Still others were blessed with private means, especially the early and slightly eccentric Roualeyn Gordon Cumming, the Scottish laird who accomplished a one-man invasion of South Africa in little more than a kilt, wearing away an inch thickness of the hardwood stock of his rifle by merely passing through hundreds of miles of heavy thorn. Of course there were also the students, the professional naturalists, and the scientists, men like C. J. P. "Iodine" Ionides, Africa's

5

snake man; wardens like Pitman, Ritchie, Stevenson-Hamilton, and Kinloch; and America's Father of Taxidermy, Carl Akeley, who, during his African experiences, was once so badly savaged by an elephant that he was given up for dead and on another occasion even had to kill a wounded leopard with his bare hands (which, nice guy or not, served him right).

It seems to me, after literally decades of researching the great Africana that has been passed down to us piled upon darn near fifteen years of my own professional hunting experience, that there is no simple answer regarding which is the most dangerous African game animal. It did and still does depend upon four factors: *When* you're speaking of; *what* terrain or field conditions pertain; *whether* the animal was wounded or provoked; and finally and most importantly, *which* of the Big Five eventually caught up with your personal baby-pink butt.

I suppose that this is as good a spot as any to attempt a general overview of what some of the Grand Masters of the sparsely wooded scrub grassland *miombo* have opined about the Big Five. Happily, most had at least one or another recorded opinion of the baddest of the bad, some even including the whole shebang in personal order of preference. Considering his rank, fresh from the White House as president of the United States, it seems not unreasonable to crank things up with one of the most obliging on the subject, Theodore Roosevelt.

Although many of his readers criticized Teddy's bully style, which was merely the reflection of a positive personality, there's little room for second guessing his opinions in *African Game Trails*. Roosevelt records with complete honesty the views of only experienced hunters and settlers, reasonably and accurately considering himself too green to voice a valid opinion as he might have had the question concerned the animals of the American West.

Roosevelt was one of the greatest admirers of Frederick Selous, whom he quotes as having killed something between three hundred and four hundred widely assorted lions, rhino, buff, and elephant by the time of his writing. Due to the relative populations of species this tally was of course broken down to "scores" of lion and rhino and "hundreds" of jumbo and buff. Despite this varied exposure, Roosevelt quotes Selous as figuring the lion to be the most dangerous, followed about evenly by the buff and the elephant—Selous had had extremely nasty tiffs with both—and trailed by the rhino. That the leopard is not even mentioned is not unusual in writings of this period, chance encounters with the slickest of the big cats being largely accidental and some of even the best African hunters largely unfamiliar with the leopard as a game species.

That the experience and hence the personal opinions of the hunters of Roosevelt's time range widely is evident in just a page or two of *African Game Trails.* Jackson, the lieutenant governor of British East Africa, is reported, based upon having killed a relatively few (eighty to ninety) of the same fearsome foursome as Selous, to have placed the buffalo "unquestionably" first, the elephant just as surely second, and the lion and rhino in the rear. Well, at least two people so far agree on the rhino. . . .

But William Henry Drummond, author of *The Large Game of Africa* and a professional hunter also mentioned by Roosevelt, made it Steuben crystal clear that the rhino was his *Numero Uno* choice for converting a hunter into a full-time rug hooker, with the lion runner-up, and the buff and the elephant trailing. Sir

7

Samuel Baker, whose opinions should be included, ranked the Big Four in order of elephant, rhino, buff, and lion. Roosevelt quotes Abel Chapman, the well-known Kenya hunter of the early 1900s, as ranking "both the elephant and the rhino as more dangerous than the lion." Teddy also remarks that ". . . many of the hunters I met in East Africa seemed inclined to rank the buffalo as more dangerous than any other animal."

Before leaving Teddy Roosevelt's comments, permit me to pass on a small allied observation of his on the relative deadliness of game species. Writing in 1909–10, Roosevelt noted that more than fifty white men had been killed or mauled by the four animals discussed during a three- to four-year period in what is now Kenya, Tanzania, and Uganda. In fact, in Nairobi he was shown the graves of seven lion-killed whites in just one churchyard cemetery. Considering that in this country there were proportionately hardly any whites compared with the indigenous blacks and Arab half-castes, this may be some indication of what is really meant by "dangerous" game. By Teddy's best guess, the lion was by far the greatest man-killer, but this may well be because of his tendency toward man-eating, which of course is limited to predators and therefore excludes buffalo, rhino, or jumbo.

The exclusion of the leopard from the ranks of dangerous game is by subsequent gory example ridiculous. In a moment, we'll get into the distinctive character of *Chui* in relation to the literal heavies with whom he deserves inclusion on the basis of meritorious mayhem. Since at the time I am punching out this book the martial arts and especially the Japanese *jutsu* forms are becoming better known in the Western world, it would be appropriate to nominate the leop-

8

ard as the *ninja*, the professional master of stealth, of the deadly African animals. It might well be that it would take three male leopards to tip the scales on a lion with a cholesterol problem, but he's pure death in the twilight, shredding you with the glee and efficiency of a coroner working—pardon the expression—on a deadline.

The point I'm getting at is that henceforth, at least in terms of this book, the Big Four has been replaced by the Big Five. This is no hog-fattening contest, and if the 25-pound honey badger killed people on a business hours basis and were a reasonable game animal, I wouldn't blink at his inclusion in the ranks, letting him make the Big Six no matter what his waistline. This is a book about hunting *dangerous* game under fair chase conditions; the "Big" and other modifiers are secondary. If you're inclined to lily gilding (mine always wilt) there are handy points of comparison that will reinforce my argument. Crocodiles kill more people in Africa than either the lion or the leopard and a big croc will make four of the biggest lions, but he is not a member of the Big Five. The hippo kills considerably more people each year than either the rhino, elephant, or buffalo, yet deserves inclusion into the quintet no more than do the cobra, mamba, tsetse fly, or snail fluke. Sure, they all kill people—in the case of the hippo with depressing consistency—but they're just not "sporting" animals. I suppose that the whole point of this extended observation is to further confirm that there *are* rules to the game.

Perhaps we ought to give a moment's consideration to what makes something dangerous in the first place. Is the most dangerous animal the one most likely to kill a hunter even though unprovoked? Or, is it the critter most difficult to follow up wounded in heavy

9

cover where the price of the sportsman's responsibility may be a rather messy job of subdivision? For example, a leopard, wounded and loitering with less than benevolent intentions in a stand of grass and thorn worse than my backyard is statistically about four times more likely to maul one or more members of the pursuing party than would a lion under identical conditions. Why? He's much smaller, faster, pound-for-pound more effective with claws and teeth (leopards use all four sets of claws, lions usually only the front), harder to hit, charges from a closer distance, and never betrays his intentions with the slightest snarl. Well, almost never.

On the other hand, although a lion will *usually* charge from a greater range, he is generally more visible and therefore a larger and easier target to hit and, further, displays the courtesy of announcing his intentions with a set of growls guaranteed to blow your jockstrap off. If you stick a big bullet into his bridgework, you'll usually get his attention and turn him; not so a leopard. *But* if a lion beats the lesser odds of reaching the hunters, he's four times more likely to actually kill at least one person rather than merely reducing the whole lot to very rare stew meat simply because his bite is so big and the damage so terrible. Hey guys, lions kill stuff like Cape buffalo with one well-placed chomp of that business end. You get grabbed through the chest with a set of those dentures and your widow can start litigation for a refund from your safari company. Incidentally, she won't get one: Reasonable risk is implied in lion hunting.

So, which is the more dangerous, the lion or the leopard? For my money, I'd rank them equal based simply on my experience as a professional. Neither one has caught up with me yet, but I've sure plugged a lot of holes in pals who've shown me how it should not be done.

Now, shifting the court's attention to the heavyweight division, I think there's a little more room for debate on the remaining terrible triumvirate—buff, rhino, and elephant—than on the cats. This might be a good time to breach the idea of the "provocation" of dangerous game. Most rhino I've bumped into—which have been far fewer than either buff or elephant— have displayed what I would only describe as a sort of implied truculence. I personally have little doubt that most rhino charges are the result of curiosity gotten out of hand through lousy eyesight and an I.Q. eight points lower than that of a standard-issue preservationist. Of course, this is sparse comfort to the hunter about to receive some 20-odd inches of horn suppository from a couple of tons of interglacial misunderstanding.

An animal does not have to have been wounded or chivied around by a hunter to be provoked to homicide. Cow elephants with young will everlastingly convince you of this, as will lions with cubs or advanced amorous ideas. It's been my conclusion that, unwounded, the rhino is slightly more inclined to charge a man than an elephant would be, but then he's far easier to avoid in average—if there is such a thing— cover. You can climb out of his way or simply use your head and avoid him. If matters get downright definite, he'll almost always turn from a shot in the kisser and take his business elsewhere.

The elephant isn't quite so accommodating. He'll bluff-charge to put you off, and exactly when a bluff turns into the genuine article will vary among elephants. If he's too close, you have six or seven tons of trouble mighty handy. A turning shot may or may not be effective with a jumbo, as I've found out as a cropping officer on several occasions.

Frankly, I personally know of not a single example of a Cape buffalo that was unhurt or that had not been fighting with other bulls or otherwise provoked to cold-bloodedly attack a human. Presumably, they have other things to keep them occupied. Still, because they are so damnably hard to kill with a single shot by a nervous, overready hunter, there are far more wounded animal situations with buffalo than with any other big game. You may be able to radically alter the aggressive attitude of nearly all rhino and most jumbo with a big-caliber belt in the chops, but make no such presumption with the buff. He has no sense of humor about such goings-on. So, as a personal appraisal, I'd have to say that the buff is the most likely to catch up with your rapidly retreating backside through sheer persistence.

A lot is made by the antihunting faction of the presumed "fact" that no animal has a chance against a modern high-powered rifle. It seems to me only fair to devote a couple of minutes to what at least appears to be a reasonable presumption. . . .

For the most part, there is not the slightest doubt that the 500-grain .458 Winchester Magnum solid bullet is a huge equalizer between man and elephant. So, asks the nonhunter, what's fair about that? Not a bad question.

The object of hunting dangerous game is only indirectly to get yourself stomped, gored, or bitten to death. In fact, it's to court the real possibility of death rather than to actually die. A humane hunter uses "enough gun" to kill quickly—hopefully instantaneously—for two reasons: first, so that the game does not have the opportunity, having been fairly

12

stalked on its own territory, to escape wounded and be wasted or lost; and second, to keep the hunter alive. Just as a rock climber doesn't use rotten rope—although it would increase the element of danger—a hunter should use enough gun not to be guilty of suicide. Lord knows, the edge of man over beast with even the most powerful of modern rifles is slight enough under the true sporting conditions typified by the hunting of dangerous game: close, dense, and restrictive cover that virtually eradicates the hunter's defenses of eyesight and hearing. After all, a bull elephant weighs about ninety times as much as a big man. No human being could begin to outrun any of the Big Five, nor would he last more than a few seconds in any contest of strength. I dislike repeating examples, but to my mind the distinction between *hunting* and *shooting* an elephant remains classic. On a bare plain, even an orangutan using open sights could leisurely shoot an elephant through the chest from two hundred yards. And why not? The target is the size of an airplane hangar wall and too far away to be remotely dangerous. Yet, at five to ten yards, to stalk up to a big tusker with a doctorate in people-pounding through bush so thick that the 14,000-pound animal is invisible, knowing that there is a chance for just one shot that will bring a sure charge if not exactly placed—that's the difference between elephant hunting and elephant killing.

That's also what big game hunting is all about.

2 BUFFALO

"FOR CHRIST'S SAKE, KILL ME!"

The agonized scream lanced the cool, shadowy air of the thicket, ending in a sobbing shriek that was washed over by the deep, savage grunts of a Cape buffalo bull. Again, the keening wail rose, then stopped abruptly in a strangled gasp. Fifty yards away, across a clearing but hidden by thick bush, a second man lay half dazed, wondering how badly his legs had been crushed by the ton of buffalo lying dead across his lower body. The thick tendrils of blood leaking from the bull's nostrils were already glazing in the mottled sunlight of the Kenyan Aberdare Range as the dust of combat settled in a thickening blanket over the glisten of fresh gore. As he lay struggling for breath, Samuel Colquhoun listened to Hunter scream again to be shot, the plea for death unanswered as the buffalo hooked a thick horn into living flesh once more and dragged the tattered half-corpse along the dead grass and dirt at the clearing's edge.

*   *   *

It was shortly after the First World War that Samuel Colquhoun, a young British officer, pitched up in the still-infant rail town of Nairobi. Full of beans from the excitement of combat, he was in search of adventure and, staying with a pal named Hunter who had a farm in Subukia, one of the most beautiful parts of Kenya's high forest country, decided to try his hand at big game hunting.

In those days, Cape buffalo herds had become a menace in the Aberdare Range as man encroached with his farms and ranches, and some of the worst trouble had occurred in the immediate vicinity of Subukia. Like the herds of elephant that had been backed into a corner by poachers, their habitat offering less and less sanctuary, the buff had also become *kali,* the KiSwahili term for aggressive or savage. Instead of melting away into the depths of their tangled haunts at the first sight of man, they had taken to routing herds of domestic cattle and had even killed several woodcutters. Big, mean, and unafraid, the buff in these herds were made to order for the presumably dashing Colquhoun and his friend, Hunter, who was no apparent relation to the professional of the same name. As soon as Colquhoun found out about the troublesome buffalo, he talked Hunter into joining him to teach them a lesson. A bit before dawn on a chilly morning in 1920, they started out with a small group of natives to hunt *Mbogo,* the Kenyan Cape buffalo.

Hunter, who should have known better, lent his spare rifle to one of the tribesmen. Perhaps the man was only meant to carry it; history is not clear. Whatever the arrangement, the party caught up with a herd of bull buffalo in an opening at the edge of the forest.

Both whites opened up on them, killing two and wounding a couple more, which disappeared into the thick woods with the rest. Without knowing much about hunting buff, the men immediately followed them into the cover, with Hunter leading and Colquhoun about ten yards back.

After some minutes, the blood spoor and tracks led through a clearing, a smallish keyhole that was surrounded by thickets. As Hunter melted from sight into the bush beyond the clearing, Colquhoun realized that somehow they had walked almost smack into the middle of the herd. As it dawned on him, he saw a charging bull bearing down on Hunter through the patches of bush. Before he could react, there was the tearing crash of a shot. The native carrying Hunter's extra rifle fired, missing the buffalo but driving a bullet through Hunter's lower back, breaking the farmer's spine. As the white man collapsed, the attacking buffalo was on him.

Colquhoun raised his rifle, trying wildly to sort out over its sights the horror of black, mud-caked hide from the bloody clothes of his friend. Before he could squeeze the trigger, an express train of shock powered into him from a blind side as another buff's horns caught him between the thighs and threw him through the air like a rag doll. The ground flipped up crazily to punch him in the face and smash the breath from his lungs. As though from a long way off, he could hear the agonized Hunter screaming as the buffalo tore him apart. As he struggled drunkenly to his feet, he could see through the bush the *Mbogo* shredding his pal with horns and hooves. His mind clearing, Colquhoun realized that two more big buffalo were staring at him with very interested expressions from a few yards

19

away. His rifle lay beyond them. He began to pray, listening as the writhing Hunter continued to plead for release from pain.

Knowing that to run would mean death, Colquhoun stood his ground. Ignoring the two immediate bulls, he cursed a strip off the buff killing Hunter, alternately shouting and waving his hands. The pair to the side, even closer than the one killing Hunter, pawed the ground in indecision, tossing heads crowned with corrugated oak bosses and looping, black, gaff-pointed horns. His attention superglued to the three buffalo facing him, Colquhoun was caught unaware by another two thousand pounds of shadowy muscle hurtling in from behind, lifting him back into space. Later, he couldn't say whether it was the bull that had tossed him the first time or another of the irritated gathering of bovine bad news. Whichever it was, the corded neck, as thick as a barrel of crude oil, threw him across the clearing as a wrist wrestler would flip a cigar butt. Samuel Colquhoun later quoted the sequence of events to a friend, who wrote it down:

What happened sounds incredible but it is the absolute truth, and I always think it was something other than sheer chance. I was flung right across the glade and landed on top of my rifle. Furthermore, it had fallen on soft ground and was undamaged; it was loaded, with the safety catch on, all ready to fire. When I had stood there seeing what was happening to Hunter I think I prayed for help. It seemed my prayer had been answered—although in a rather peculiar way. Anyhow, I had the rifle, and that changed the whole situation for me.

20

Brother, count on that!

As Colquhoun was soaring through the air, the bull that had launched him the second time probably lost sight of his orbiting carcass. When Colquhoun landed, though, it spotted him and thundered over to finish the job. It was nearly on him by the time he could get the rifle out from under his aching body and reverse it, pushing a lucky bullet through the bull's brain. It was not too little but, as I know from having had the same thing happen to me, a mini-second too late. The dead weight of nearly a ton of defunct buffalo collapsed across his legs, pinning the battered man to the ground with its ponderous head and shoulders. Anchored as if under a concrete buttress, Colquhoun could only listen to Hunter continue screaming for somebody to come and kill him, although heaven knows that the buff above him was doing its best.

The rest of the herd had left, only the *Mbogo* rearranging Hunter remaining at the far side of the glade. Colquhoun screeched bloody murder for the Africans and, to what would have been the general surprise of most experienced hunters, they came back. With sticks and saplings, they levered the dead buff off Colquhoun's legs, although the bull only a few dozen yards away was still in business. Sam managed to get to his feet and bravely stagger over and kill Hunter's tormentor. Temporary truce.

With a bullet through his lower spine and the horrible damage done by the buffalo, it was practically Ripley's material that Hunter was even remotely alive. One good look, however, indicated that he would not be so for much longer. Poles were cut and a hammock made out of the Africans' blankets to carry Hunter back to his farmhouse. It was a long walk to the edge of the cultivated fields, with plenty of evidence of still greatly displeased buffalo on either side of the route. The toughest part was that, despite his awful injuries, Hunter did not pass out from the pain, perhaps because he had been gored and pummeled for so long that his adrenaline was up. The agony was unbearable, especially when the carriers had to stop and rest the hammock on the forest floor. Just before Hunter's own fields were reached, the mangled, dying man decided not to bear it any further. Colquhoun, who knew how bad the injuries were from both bullet and bull, was relieved. He never hunted again.

The story of Colquhoun and Hunter is by no stretch an unusual one except that after having been tossed twice and with incredible luck having been hit by the curve of the horns rather than turned into shish kebab on the points, Colquhoun survived to tell the tale—and relive it in his nightmares—with no really serious injuries. The point is that wounded buff are definitely to be avoided, which ain't always easy, for they take so much killing.

Buffalo are almost unique in their bullet resistance, hardly wincing at what would flatten most other members of the Big Five, including rhino. In a charge, the great majority of elephants will turn from a face or head shot, as will the rhino. The cats, lion and leopard, are nowhere near as bulletproof as the other three, with the pachyderms' massive musculature and thick skins. Still, the buff is really alone in his resolve to carry through a charge once started.

There are two current production models of buffalo in Africa, not to mention a couple of Indian or Asian varieties that could not be classified as compacts. The heavy hitter of the lot is the Cape buffalo, *Syncerus caffer,* who is found from East Africa down into the Republic of South Africa, with numerous interesting stops in between. *Rowland Ward's Records of Big Game* (17th ed., 1977) lists fifty-two subspecies of probably debatable validity, although I would certainly agree that there are several types of Cape buff exemplified by different regions.

Africa's other buffalo is the so-called bush cow or dwarf buffalo, which differs greatly in appearance from his southern relative, being much smaller, hairier, redder in color, and with quite dissimilar horn conformation. I am familiar, through other authors, with his reputation for ferocity because of what may be some sort of Napoleon Complex, but I have never hunted his territory, which ranges from central Africa, Chad, and Zaire westward into the Atlantic countries. Frankly, I could care less, as they are rarely hunted by sportsmen today, much of their range having taken on the distinct carmine hue of emerging Communist nations, which don't seem to like Western hunters poking around their boondocks. In any case, I can't imagine that anyone who has hunted the hulking, scowling, and thoroughly sporting southern buffalo would ever want to switch affections to the bush cow, as nasty as he at times can reportedly be. That would be rather like jilting Dolly Parton in favor of Little Orphan Annie. So let's confine our discussion to the big, bad one, who will tip in at an average of about seventeen hundred pounds and as much as twenty-two hundred pounds for a bull who's not watching his calories.

Most hunters would agree that Cape buffalo are big, but you've just got no idea how big until you get into heavy cover with one that has decided he doesn't like the cut of your coat. Buff are highly inconsiderate once their dander is up, regularly shrugging off major holes in their exteriors that would stall an armored personnel carrier. There is no rationing on dander when it comes to *Inyati,* probably because their irritability with fumble-fingered hunters is expressed in pure adrenaline. This is translated into the following formula: $B + LS = F$. For the uninitiated, this means Buff + Lousy Shot = Funeral. Excellent historical precedent indicates that it will be yours.

Like anything else, buff are not *really* bulletproof, despite every indication to the contrary. If you perforate them properly with adequate bullets (one shot per customer, please) they will go floomph! into a dark heap and never register the slightest displeasure. The problem arises when the hunter realizes the potential consequences and whiffs the shot, rather like the difference between tapping in a 4-foot putt on the practice range and completing the same stroke when you're tied for the U.S. Open and are putting for a birdie.

Although the phenomenon is to some degree shared by all the Big Five, no member of the quintet makes as much use as the buffalo of such glandular excretions as adrenaline. Possibly he's just the right size and of the proper construction; I really don't know. One would figure the elephant to be tough through sheer size, but on any basis, I'd far rather argue with a gut-shot jumbo than a buff. Furthermore, there are far more wounded buffalo than elephant on a given safari because the vital target is much smaller and is usually obscured partially by cover and because the excellent combined senses of the buff require the shot to be taken at much greater ranges than in the case of elephant.

The point is that if a buff isn't cooled on the first go (unless badly lung-shot, which will take a bit longer), he'll be a dozen times tougher to put down than on the first try. Also, he'll be ready for you, and buff really know how to get ready.

Wounded buff almost always head directly downwind so that they can't be followed up without their scenting the pursuer, and it is equally axiomatic that they seek cover, the nastiest, thorniest, most snarled backlash of bush available. Once nice and snug in this mess, they settle down and wait, perhaps lying down so that they're invisible, but often standing up, poised and equally camouflaged by the bush breaking their outline. When they've got you nice and zeroed in as closely as possible, they'll open the festivities.

The unusual aspect of the buff is that, of the three really big dangerous species, he has no weak spots in his natural defenses. He has the eyesight of a cheetah, the hearing of a hypertensive elephant, and the smelling ability of a bird dog on a damp morning. In bush, he can do anything better than you can, including running at four times your speed through cover so dense that it would make a mole claustrophobic.

Handling a buffalo charge is about as dangerous as things get in Africa. Of course, that takes nothing from either lion or leopard, but at least if you punch either of them in the chest with something appropriate, you'll hurt or kill them, in both cases stopping the charge. Not *Mbogo*. You can hand him a half-pound of high-velocity how-de-doo right where the Monongahela meets the Allegheny and he will politely grunt at you while increasing speed.

Again, it's adrenaline. As has often been discussed, buff have a phenomenal talent for storing oxygen in their brains under stress or in pain, which delays the effect of even a perfect heart shot under the luckiest of circumstances up to a minute or more. It doesn't take all that much imagination to figure out what a Cape buffalo bull—or cow, for that matter—can do to a human body over the period of a television commercial, despite the fact that the bloody thing may have no more than the equivalent of a pulverized grapefruit where its ticker used to be.

Buffalo charge with their heads well up and forward, completely unlike fighting bulls. The horns are only dropped at the split second before impact, making the brain shot about as feasible for most shooters as picking off a flying hummingbird with a derringer while blindfolded and drunk. When in what is now Zimbabwe some years ago, I had a good look at a buffalo skull that had been sawn down the middle between the horns. Even I, who on expeditions never seemed to have a saw, was surprised to see how low the brain itself lies in the head, perfectly protected by the horn boss and by the entire bone structure of the face. In fact, I still marvel that over my career to date I have been able to kill the half-dozen or so buff that have frontally charged me, so tough is the angle. Actually, I almost surely *didn't* kill them with a bullet to the brain by shooting at the nostrils but was close enough to put them into terminal coma until the insurance shot could be administered. Incidentally, my axiom is "If it bites, put out its lights." Don't *ever* take a chance with the big stuff; shoot it again *no matter how certain* you are that it's dead. This applies in particular to buff and elephant. What's the cost of a bullet compared with your hospital bills, and that only if you're lucky?

Even professionals have propounded some very interesting theories on how to stop charging buff. One, espoused by a couple of well-known writers of yore (I know, I know; what's yore? Scotch, thanks very much), calls for letting the Sedan de Ville–sized wounded buff get close enough—a few feet—to drop his head, at which point the icy calm hunter nails him down through the withers, breaking the spine *et al.* I can assure you that anybody who lets a wounded buff get that close to him on purpose is in need of suicide prevention counseling. As far as I am concerned, I prefer to shoot them in the eye region or the bridge of the nose, where a well-placed slug will disrupt even a determined buff to the extent that a man can have a shot at something a bit more substantial, such as the back of the neck or the shoulder, if he's quick on his feet. True, often buff can be stopped by being literally broken down with chest shots that angle off and break shoulders or, if you're a praying man, maybe even a piece of spine, but I reckon the odds too dicey. A perfect shot where the body joins the throat or neck is usually very effective on unwounded buffalo that are facing you, perhaps trying to figure out what you are through the bush, but that doesn't reckon with the adrenaline and determination of a winged one. Still, from maybe fifty yards or more, if following up a cripple and offered that shot, I'd take it if I were sure of being able to get off a couple more at the head when or if he got in close.

Somebody once observed that, incredibly, a buff with a broken foreleg or shoulder seemed to move faster in a charge than does one without such a presumed disadvantage. I wholeheartedly agree, and further concur that the reason is probably the pain of the broken leg swinging free. Whether or not it would be equally true in the matter of a broken hind leg I don't know, as I can't recall having ever played pop goes the weasel with one sporting such an injury.

Beyond reason of trophy damage, I wouldn't suggest the head shot at an unwounded buff from a broadside angle but would rather advise the shoulder. The heart lies very low in the body, too much so for my taste, although a bullet above it will do most unsavory things to the arteries and big veins as well as disrupting the forward lung area. I discovered what is invariably my favorite broadside shot pretty much by accident when hunting with Bob Gill of Fort Lauderdale, Florida, on a safari in the Luangwa Valley of Zambia (formerly Northern Rhodesia). We had stalked a group of four or five carefree bachelors, one of them with an especially fine wingspan of horns. Lord, but he was a big bull in the body, too, simply hunching up a bit and taking off across our front at about fifty yards without showing any real effect of Bob's perfect bullet placement, right through the top of the heart and into the skin of the far side. Of course, I didn't know that at the moment and, seeing that he was heading for a very dense clump of riverine bush, decided to give him a little more ballast while things were still on my terms. I swung on him, touched off the .375 H&H, and couldn't believe my eyes when he dropped as if electrocuted, without so much as a twitch. Actually, it was so unusual to see an *Njati* almost blow up in flames that I wondered if he'd fallen into one of the deep gullies cut near the river by the rainy season floods and now obscured by 3-foot growth. Nope, he was as dead as the penny postcard right where he had fallen, my bullet having entered above and to the left of Bob's as the bull ran to our right. Of course, I had spined him, and with a smashed upper spinal column, not much of anything goes anywhere.

I performed a bit of an autopsy while the headskin and meat were being taken by my men and found the most convenient aspect of the shot is that the spine lies exactly one-third of the way down from the top of the line of the shoulder, a nice, easy guidepost. With a chance for a solid rest on a stationary animal, I have favored this shot ever since, and only rarely has it been less than instantly fatal. If a smidgen low, it will break the shoulder complex; low and back, the lungs catch the slug. Another advantage of the spine shot is that you can tell immediately if it's been properly placed, whereas with heart or lung shots, the animal can move around quite a bit before the bullet takes effect. If the buff doesn't drop to the shot, there's usually time to rake him through the chest before he's off and gone.

One drawback to the spine shot, though, is that, like braining an elephant, the bullet may pass close enough to glance and stun, making the hunter think that the beast is being reasonable. Again, always pay the insurance. Buffalo can get up in one hell of a hurry and, if they catch you, the stuff on what is left of your face will be a lot more than egg. . . .

There are times when the solid bullet, although preferred for its penetration, is inappropriate on buffalo. I rank it with three hundred grains of the True Cross for hunting big, lone bulls, but when there are others around, such as typically overlapping in a herd, there's the danger of the bullet's going completely through the target animal and wounding a second. If I were meat or sport hunting rather than backing up a client, I'd carry as the first round in the chamber a good, tough soft-point, perhaps a Winchester Silvertip or a Remington Core-Lokt, and stack the rest of the magazine with solids. Using a double, I normally opt for one barrel of soft-point and the other of solid.

I've written in both *Death in the Long Grass* and

Death in the Silent Places of some of my more memorable experiences with Cape buffalo, including what it feels like to have one in your lap (*very* heavy). I've also told the tale of my idea of spearing one African-style and how nearly, but for the quick shooting by a pal, I came to eternal bliss. Among the other brushes I've had with *Inyati,* there is another that I will not likely forget in any great hurry, and that was more than a dozen years ago.

I was hunting out of Mwangwalala Camp on the Luangwa and had noticed the spoor of a big tom leopard crossing the hunting track. Interested to see if we could find a natural kill somewhere nearby that we might use as a setup for the safari starting the next day, my gunbearer Silent and I walked very quietly for a mile or so away from the river, just keeping our eyes open. I was carrying my .375 slung over my shoulder but shifted it to my hands as we edged through a section of extremely thick and leafy bush at the top of a long, dry, washed-out gully. I was actually down on my hands and heels in a sort of squat, trying to get past a thornbush, when I looked up. Fewer than five *feet* away was a very large eye, looking through me like a laser. The animal was so close that I couldn't even recognize what it was, although I knew that it sure was big! For less than a second, I looked at it and it looked back. There was no hope of bringing my rifle to bear; hell, had it been in position I could actually have touched the beast with its muzzle! At the same instant I gave a gargled grunt of shock, the bush exploded into thundering motion. Rolling, I yelled at Silent, who was behind me, to run. I was so frightened and surprised that I actually thought I was having a heart attack, but, when the sound got a bit farther away, I realized that it wasn't coming at me. When we got our blood pressure back on the scale, we had a look and saw that it had been a lone buffalo bull, who must have been asleep in the shade of the thicket, not waking until he looked into my eyeball with the same sentiments I had felt looking into his. If he hadn't decided to run but had charged, I wouldn't have had the chance of a Colonel Sander's chicken of getting out of his way.

For all their ferocity when aroused or wounded, buff are usually not inclined to go looking for trouble. Of course, the rub in this lies in the fact that one can't tell if a buffalo lying up in cover is nursing lion injuries, gore wounds from fighting with other bulls, or poacher-inflicted damage. If he's in a black mood, he doesn't much care who caused the unpleasantness and will charge out, murder in his eyes, without regard to color, race, creed, or national origin. Buff have been known to disembowel motor vehicles when in less than a jolly frame of mind. I am also personally aware of one crusty old boy who single-handedly killed three lions, two females and a male, although he died a few hours later from his wounds. An angry buff can do a memorable job on a horse, too.

Frederick Selous had an interesting time of it in Rhodesia back around the turn of the century when he spotted the tracks of two big bulls and gave chase. Getting within range on horseback, Selous had two misfires from his muzzle loader after dismounting and then remounted to approach within forty yards to shoot from the saddle. His horse, usually reliable, refused to stand still and instead began to walk *toward* the glowering buff as if he weren't there. Unable to hold steady for a shot, yet without time to grab the dropped reins, Selous found the buff and his horse on a collision course as he fired at a mere six feet from the bull's nose. As his old gun at last went off, the buff was in full charge.

Selous slammed his spurs into the horse's flank, but there was never a hope. The big *Inyati* smashed into the mount with the full impact of its one-ton-plus of irritation, "pitching it," Selous recounted later, "with me on its back, into the air like a dog. The recoil of the heavily-charged elephant gun with which I was shooting twisted it clean out of my hands, so that we all, horse, gun and man, fell in different directions."

Selous had missed! That he had may have saved his life.

The horse ran off, trailing most of its insides outside, and had to be destroyed when the hunter finally caught up with it. Selous, though, had other matters on his mind at the moment. A few feet away, the buffalo looked at him, gave a grunt, and charged him again.

I threw my body out flat along the ground and just avoided the upward thrust of his horn, receiving, however, a severe blow on the left shoulder with the round part of it; nearly dislocating my right arm with the force with which my elbow was driven against the ground; and received a kick on the instep from one of his feet. Luckily, he did not turn again, as he most certainly would have done had he been wounded, but galloped clean away.

William Finaughty recorded another incident (among many) in which a young man named Blanch had borrowed a fine hunting horse, valued at seventy-five pounds, from one Mr. Hudson. In company with

Finaughty, the men were not even hunting but returning the horse when, from the rear of the bush through
which they were traveling, a bull buff came charging.
Finaughty was able to kill the bull before it started to
dissect Blanch, but the horse looked as if it had been
through an early model food processor. Young
Blanch, who didn't have the kind of money that seventy-five pounds represented in those days, had to live
with the black embarrassment of the loss.

Should you get the idea that it's necessary to go
back years to find a proper buffalo incident, let me
suggest the case of Bruce McIvor, who is still undergo-
ing plastic surgery and skin grafting.

It was the morning of October 24, 1981, less than a
year before the time of this writing. Bruce, a naturalist, was in the Caprivi Strip on a busman's holiday
with his family. Caprivi is the little geopolitical spit of
territory that connects what used to be German South-
west Africa (now South-West Africa and called by
some factions Namibia) with the Zambezi watershed,
a little finger of territory between Botswana on the
south and Angola and Zambia on the north. A thin,
blue ink line on the map, the Cuando River divides
Caprivi into left and right halves, and it was on the
Cuando that Bruce and his family were camped on a
warm Saturday morning.

The whining of Cindy, his personal pooch, mixed
with the vocal indigestion of hippos, the glass-edged
shriek of fish eagles, and the haunting velvet calls of
laughing doves awoke McIvor and his wife. As usual,
he went out first to make the coffee. In the casual
camp, besides his wife and two sons, were his father,
then seventy-nine; a friend and his wife; and another
dog. It was to be a fishing weekend, spincasting the
Cuando's deep, slick-surfaced pools and foaming

33

roiled riffles for African bream and an occasional ti-
gerfish, the *Tilapia* bream to provide the succulent filets for a dinner *braai* cookout and the tigers to provide
the slashing, leaping fight that only a set of beartrap
teeth propelled by a striped, streamlined body could
offer a sportsman.

With a receding line of light brown hair, McIvor is
built with the residual power of the savage *sjambok*
whip, cut from raw hippo hide and thin, supple, but as
terrible as steel. In his late thirties, he is as flexible
and muscular as men in their early twenties. McIvor is
not one you would want to fool with.

The sun was glaring down by half-past eight when,
breakfast finished, the whole camp moved out to fish,
even the dogs permitted to run through the scattered
bush along the Cuando. Big mistake.

The fishing was lousy. At half-past twelve, when the
party met for a lunch campfire meal of beef and sau-
sages they had luckily brought along, not a fish had
been taken, although young Sean McIvor, aged nine,
had lost a good one just before lunch. Under the scald-
ing October sun of Caprivi, naps didn't have to be or-
dered at gunpoint. The sun, arcing in the Southern
Hemisphere from east to north to west, was well past its
zenith when the fishing resumed at around two.

Frustrated, Bruce decided to wander farther upriver
than usual to a very promising pool he knew of, although it had never produced any cookout material.
Still, if Sean had hooked a good one a bit before, perhaps the feeding cycle was on. To his surprise, Bruce
landed two good bream in successive casts and gave a
shout to the rest of the group, leaving the pool to
them while he pushed even farther upstream. As he
walked, studying the swirling waters, he heard the two
dogs barking in the bush. Knowing that numerous lion

and leopard were found along the Cuando, Bruce McIvor whistled for them to come to heel. At the same time, he noticed a couple of very fishy spots he hadn't tried before. His attention diverted from the dogs ahead, he moved on another fifty yards. To reach the promising spots, he saw that he would have to squeeze by a thornbush that grew smack down to the water's edge. He was halfway around it when he began the ordeal of his life.

"As I rounded the thornbush, I heard a heavy crashing and a deep grunting in the bushes just ahead of me," he wrote to a close mutual friend. "The next thing the two dogs came streaking toward and past me with an old buffalo bull charging about twenty yards behind them, most upset at having his afternoon siesta disturbed." With a wealth of hunting experience, Bruce McIvor realized that he was in big trouble. Still, even though unarmed, he froze between the edge of the bush and the water, presuming that the buff was after the dogs and not him.

Wrong. Looking over his shoulder and "seeing the buffalo coming after me, I realized that I was in grave danger." Lordie, you can say that in lights!

Bruce realized, as had Selous previously, that his only chance with nothing to climb was to lie down. He knew that the odds of his being trampled were substantial but it was his only option. Nobody outruns a buffalo. Preferring the hooves to the awful horns, he took his own advice. Things didn't work out very well.

As buffalo and man came together, Bruce was lying with his feet toward the bull and thumped the animal in the face, yet with no result, as he had no real leverage. Not that he would have been remotely able to fend it off had he been wearing razor-honed ice skates. It got past his feet and began trying to gore him in the legs, slashing in savage, black sweeps with the meathooks on its head. McIvor looked wildly about and grabbed a fallen piece of deadwood some ten inches thick and nine feet long, trying to protect his groin. The buff whacked this several times and then ran around the man, grunting like a bass organ the whole time, until it knelt on Bruce's right side and tried once more to stick him with the terrible black horns. McIvor knew enough about buffalo to realize that if he couldn't get the animal off him, it would be only a matter of seconds before he was dead meat.

Again, McIvor kicked the bull in the nose, which only infuriated the animal further. With a hooking wrench it drove a horn deep into the man's right leg, just below the knee. Convinced that he was as good as dead, Bruce McIvor decided to go down swinging.

Desperate, he made a grab across his own body for the bull's left horn with his left hand. Missed. Again, and he felt the smooth, steel hardness under his calloused fingers. Without a thought, he stabbed his right index finger into the gray and red-rimmed left eye glaring over him, feeling it sink in up to the knuckle without much resistance. There was absolutely no reaction, which sent a chill of renewed terror through McIvor. A second, even more vicious poke in the eye brought results. With a grunt of pain, the bull tore his horn out of Bruce's leg and stepped back. He stood up, turned, and ran off. The buff wasn't twenty yards into the cover before Bruce realized that it was heading directly for the lower pool where the other six members of the party were fishing. Screaming a warning to his elderly dad, his wife, and the children, he bounced to his feet despite his badly bleeding gore wound, running after the animal that had mauled him. Happily, he didn't catch the bull. After one hundred yards, he realized that the buff was going to stay in the thicket along the river, for its crashing had stopped.

Mrs. McIvor was first on the scene as Bruce's fishing pal went to get the Land Rover a quarter mile away. McIvor remembers shouting for help, only to be glad later that it had not come. The only weapon with the party was a .38 Special revolver, not much of a buffalo-stopper. For all Bruce knows, that bull is still in the thicket by the pool on the Cuando.

The wound in McIvor's leg was six inches deep. The horn had not passed completely through, as would be consistent with its curve, but had torn free when the bull jerked away from the second stab in its eye to leave a terrible oblong crater in the flesh below McIvor's right knee. Bruce finally ended up in the hospital in Pretoria, South Africa, where the wound required nearly six weeks of initial treatment. Plastic surgery and skin grafts are planned for the future. His advice? "Always go armed with enough gun."

Today, the buffalo is the one member of the Big Five at which a sport hunter may be almost certain to have a crack, depending, of course, upon what area of Africa he chooses to hunt. The lion is always iffy, as the leopard can be. Elephants are far from rare items, but a man may not wish to spend the hunting fee required by the government to collect one that is not very long in the tooth. Rhino, as we'll discuss, are very carefully conserved and frightfully expensive. But the buff is definitely on the increase, not only in numbers but in habitat area.

In the 1890s, a terrible outbreak of the dread cattle disease rinderpest swept across East Africa, eventually spreading all the way down to the South African cape, crossing the Zambezi in 1895. Of course, the splithooved game suffered incredibly; reliable veterinary estimates of the survival rate among Cape buff throughout their range were put at only a tiny fraction of one percent! Yet, such is the resiliency of the species that, by 1912, the herds were considered by those who had seen them before the outbreak to be back to their regular numbers!

Today, despite the closing of some excellent buffalo areas to foreigners and/or hunters, the Cape buff is in excellent shape as a classic game animal. Zimbabwe, Botswana, Zambia, and South Africa all have good populations both on ranch-owned lands and in hunting concessions.

If anything, buffalo hunting is quite a bit more dangerous today than it was. Whereas the buff used ordinarily to water in broad daylight, as they still do in some parks where they're unmolested, it's far more common to see them only near dawn or dark, coming out of or going into heavy cover where they spend their days, emerging to feed only at night. This obviously means close-range hunting conditions, and the closer one is to a buffalo or even a couple of hundred of them, the closer one is to major trouble.

Quite a few of the old-time writers mentioned "mass charges" by buffalo herds, which were in every instance I have researched merely the misinterpretation of someone who got in the way of a panicked herd. Naturally, the prospect of perhaps 200,000 pounds of wild sirloin thundering down on anybody should be reckoned with some foreboding, yet this is not a genuine gang attack or for damned sure nobody would have been around to have written about it. I have been in at least six such rushes, once at night with Bob Langeveld on a cropping exercise that was mentioned in *Death in the Long Grass*. In fact, the herds will go out of their way to avoid a man if he waves his hands and shouts over the incredible noise, normally flowing around him the way water does a rock in a stream current. It takes, shall we say, a firm constitution not to run, but I've never heard of anybody actually hurt in a buffalo stampede if he knew what he was doing and kept his nerve.

The problem is the individual animal. Buffalo packing headgear worth collecting are rarely found in herds, although this does vary from location to location, for sometimes a good bull can be found in a mess of cows and calves. But for the most part the better heads are in the bachelor clubs, little bunches of non-libbers that run anywhere from a single, cantankerous, horn-worn elder to as many as fifteen males. The best bull I ever saw, with horns at least fifty inches in spread and as thick as barn beams, was on the Munyamadzi Flats in Zambia. My client and I hunted him for two days before he and his pals exited frolicking for good, and we never got a shot, although on three occasions we were within thirty yards. He was as smart as he was big, and although the hyenas have pulled him down by now unless a very capitalistic lion got lucky, I'll always see him looming like a very bad illustration in a pulp magazine.

Really fine buffalo trophies are generally from bulls that are on the verge of becoming old. Come to think of it, the buffalo is the only member of the Big Five with horns, which grow over a central core of porous, blood-transmitting bone and tissue. Unlike deer, which shed their antlers each year, horns are permanent fixtures that reach an optimum length and then begin to wear down. The armaments of an old bull, which have been under a few years of abrasion by bush and dirt, will be less well balanced than will those of a slightly younger bull who is still past maturity. They are, however, classic overkill weapons when it comes to sticking items through the guts of the incautious or careless.

Today, there are really two kinds of buffalo hunting: the search for a really fine trophy head among the gentlemen's clubs and the sorting out of a good but perhaps less than record-book chap from a herd. Neither pastime is lacking in excitement.

The hunting of herds tends to be the more stimulating to the endocrine system; there've been times that I wished I were wearing rubber BVDs, although the classic chase of a few old and wise hatrack types may appeal more to the precision stalker and is hardly dull. Normally, the spoor of the smaller herds is picked up as it crosses a hunting track or other clear ground, giving some idea of the size of the bunch, the number of bulls, and the approximate time of their passing by the drying of the surface of the dung. Given the sight, hearing, smell, and sheer number of the buff, getting close enough to do something unsociable to a decent male is one of the tougher hunting techniques. Should you be under the impression that walking *into* a herd of buffalo as they're resting and waiting until the one you've picked is close enough even though you're surrounded by the others is for the casual aficionado, I suggest that you stick with cottontail rabbits.

The sensation of edging past loafing buffalo and examining them at fifteen or so yards for horn quality is nightmarish; in fact, when in this situation I always wonder what the hell I'm doing there. In the thick crud, shots will be bloody close, and after the stunned silence of an anemic half-second, the immediate explosion of tons upon tons of hurtling charcoal-to-buff bodies at least *should* scare you. It certainly does me! Twice I have had to put down other herd members with frontal shots when they realized that they were so close that they pretty well had to charge. Usually, though, if an anthill, or more properly a termite heap, is handy, the rest of the herd will just rush by, but it would not be a very good place to trip over your shoelace. Over the years, I have been comforted by the presence of large trees nearly as much as by termite heaps.

A frill that can be added to this form of the sport, though I wouldn't care to try it with the bachelor groups, is charging the herd instead of the other way around. Of course, a professional can't do this with every client, but if a hunter is fit and reasonably dumb, has prepaid his safari, and does not have small children or major creditors, this is one of the best hunting tactics that can be employed on buffalo.

The scenario would run as follows: You have spooked a herd, perhaps seventy-five strong, with a decent bull. A cow, who was lying down unseen, jumped up practically at your feet and rushed off. With everything else but a hearty Hi Ho, Silver, the rest followed her. They went, of course, downwind. After the equivalent of a nonstop double decathlon, with a half-hour allowed for the herd to slow up, you have managed to get in front of them, the wind now in your favor. They're walking, stirring up that unforgettable backlighted dust as they wander along, not feeding yet but holding to a solid track that will bring them about thirty yards past the fallen snarl of dead tree where you and your hunter are hiding. Your heart threatens to crack the glasses in your breast pocket as they pass in a thick dark tendril, glaring suspiciously at your hiding place. Then, the bull you have an appointment with shows—naturally—on the far side of the herd, shielded by the rest. If you want him, there's only one thing to do. Just be sure you want him *very* much.

Your *bwana* grips your shoulder, holding his rifle in his left hand. "Come on, goddammit!" he yells at the top of his lungs. He has excellent lungs. The buffalo freeze. So do you. You may be dumb, but you're certainly not stupid. Still, in a blur of movement, you're dodging past assorted bovines, shrieking like a demon with a hotfoot. Buffalo—*Cape* bloody buffalo—look at you in the purest astonishment. Ha! And they think *they're* surprised! Then, like a pop-up target, he's right in front of you, ten yards away, just swinging his head to the side as he starts off. You stick the big foresight into its notch with the rear, and without thinking the whole thing is lined up on the rippling muscles of the boulderlike shoulder. Wham! Whock! The bull stumbles. The action is as smooth as 40-year old scotch as another round slides home and the bolt is palmed over. The buff starts to turn, loses his balance, and winds up in a pile like a kid on roller skates. Up comes the head, the horns curved and gleaming as the mandibles of a giant, hairy tarantula. Then a sound is heard, a sound that must be earned. It begins low and crescendoes, a terrible, wonderful, awful yet magnificent death song, a rising bellow that washes over the bush in its finality. The head drops and he's gone. He's also yours forever.

He's still warm when you finish your cigarette and the black skinning crew comes up, but the ticks already know. Red and gorged, abandoning ship, they're crawling off the scrotum to wander away in the dry grass, seeking another host. The professional's steel tape slithers out and marks the spread at a whisper past forty-two inches, a good bull with a boss that nearly meets in the center, leaving only a slender part between the two halves like a fresh haircut. The white edge of the bullet hole in the incredibly thick skin of the scarred shoulder is just right, the bones beneath broken, the big bullet a lump you will later cut out from beneath the hide of the offside. Bent and discolored, it will be put into the little box in your desk drawer along with the lion's "lucky" floating collar bones, the flint scraper picked up where some hominid must have dropped it unthinkable hundreds of centuries ago, the dried black and red thumb-sized seeds of the mahogany tree knocked down by Silent's slingshot, and the chunk of stream-washed quartz crystal that turned out not to be the new Kohinoor Diamond after all. To anybody else it would be just another twisted chunk of scrap lead and cuprous metal. To you it's as grand a memory as the big, glaring, shoulder mount with thorn-tattered ears over the fireplace in the den, in the presence of which none of your pals seems to discuss the size of the monstrous whitetail deer he outwitted last season or the ferocity of the black bear he collected in the Poconos. Fifty times, over the years, you'll weigh that slug in your hand, examine the rifling marks, and marvel at the I-beam bone that bent it into a U. Fifty times you'll almost take it to be made into a keyring, but you'll never get around to it. And you and I both know that you never will. It's far better off in that private little shrine that all hunters have in their desk drawers, along with the aluminum bands from far-wandering black ducks and the fossils and arrowheads of our youth. I suppose it's the way of hunters. We are very odd fellows.

Should you be contemplating a safari to acquire a

good buff, please be advised that the normal sequence of events is seldom as simple as the foregoing. A trophy buffalo is rare and envied because it has an intrinsic value generated by the most stringent rules of both commerce and emotion. All things, including buffalo heads, are valuable to their owners in direct proportion to the cost, difficulty, or danger involved in obtaining them. Buffalo are paid for in the Churchillian liquid commodities as well as by pure lucre. There will certainly be sweat on the bill; if things get tricky and tough, perhaps tears. If you are unlucky, it may be blood: yours.

I would hate to have to decide which is the greatest potential confrontation between the hunter in Africa and the Big Five, but I think few would suggest that hunting bull buffalo groups or lone individuals would not rank high. It takes nothing from the hunting of the herds; it's just that things are a bit more personal when tracking an individual, particularly a scabby old sorehead such as a lone buff.

That these loners are generally the biggest of the clan is demonstrated by the fact that alone or even with a few pals they defy lions. They're smart, tough, and don't back off when push comes to shove. They don't move around like the herds, having a greater sense of territory, and are thus completely familiar with every blade of grass and twig in their area. They're bad enough to catch up to when they're being cute, but if they become wounded, things have a way of getting worse. Some of the greatest hunting confrontations have involved buffalo that are aroused or hurt. Perhaps a typical one is that of ivory hunter Marcus Daly, who had a real humdinger.

Daly had been hunting buffalo in the Aberdares of

44

Kenya on free license, near a place called Rumuruti, with two Boer brothers, Danny and Albert Loeis. Working with ponies and dogs, the hunters were trying to thin out the highly touchy buff while turning a buck on their hides and meat. On a day that Daly went out on his own and killed five buffalo with the .416 Rigby that he also favored for elephant, the Loeis boys had had a scary experience with a huge lone bull that had chased them off without their firing a shot when the two had tracked it down into thick bush. Why neither of the hunters, both with fine reputations as marksmen, had plugged the old boy is unclear, but they were convinced that the presence of such a fire-breather in the hunting area would sooner or later lead to big problems. In fact, sooner. So the next morning, all three men were off on the track at dawn, accompanied by three local tribesmen and two dogs.

As they neared the place where the buffalo had been the day before, a good black rhino bull popped up and somebody fired, wounding it. The rhino ducked back into the dense cover and was gone before he could be decked. Leaving the blacks, the three hunters loosed the dogs and went in after the rhino, Albert Loeis leading, followed by Marcus Daly and Danny Loeis. On the old game path, the bush was terrifically thick and visibility practically zero, but only a few yards inside, the men found a spreading pool of fresh blood and—of all things—the track of the big rogue buff atop it. At this moment, the dogs sounded off one hundred yards farther on, and the men pushed forward cautiously, knowing that there were two dangerous animals in the thicket. After only ten paces, a splintering of brush sounded directly ahead and Albert, who was apparently no dope, took a flying slide under a protective thornbush, leaving Daly standing in the path. The instant that Albert Loeis disappeared, his shape was replaced by that of a gigantic buffalo bull tearing flat-out at Daly.

There was no time for Daly to duck or throw himself aside as the bull hurtled forward. Jerking his rifle up, Daly fired at point-blank, the animal almost towering over him. The buff tossed his head and caught the rifle as it went off, tearing it out of Daly's grip and literally throwing it into the trees over his head. The hunter was smashed flat as the neck and front of the bull's chest crushed into him with terrible force.

As Daly came to his shocked senses, all he could see was buffalo hide above him. Realizing that his shot had stunned the bull, he dared not move for fear that he would bring the animal to its senses, yet it stood directly over him, perhaps to recover at any second. Snared by the wait-a-bit thorns he had dived into, Albert was helpless to rescue him. Danny had cut and run, now long out of sight back down the trail. Daly had a lovely close-up of the animal that would probably kill him, as blood ran off the wounded bull's nose from the bullet hole located an inch from the center of the boss and a touch high. Still dopey from the impact of the blow that had left him feeling like a sack full of broken glass, it occurred to Daly that the buff might well die and fall, pulping the man beneath him.

His nostrils full of the reek of buffalo, sweet but wild, the man watched the big bull start to sway back and forth over his body. Half unconscious from being struck, Daly struggled to move as the buff picked up its right forefoot, the cloven hoof as broad and sharp as a flatiron. He managed to move a bit as the hoof, suspended right over his head, thumped back down and just grazed him, the thud of its landing ringing loud in his ears. A burst of pain flashed up his body as the animal's left hind foot came down on his right knee, glancing off as the bull came to another stop with Daly underneath and parallel, his head directly under the bull's chin.

For the centuries that Daly lay under the buffalo, wondering if he would be crushed or stamped to death, Danny Loeis had been creeping back, and now he saw his friend's predicament. Afraid to shoot, Danny stood gape-mouthed until at last the bull took a few more steps without touching Daly and the man was clear. So shaken was Loeis that, although practically on top of the buffalo, he shot it through the stomach. But it was enough. The great bull staggered a few steps and fell over, sounding the awesome death bellow.

Marcus Daly had another experience that's worth noting, although it involved neither personal risk nor first-person confrontation. In what was then Rhodesia, hunting along the Nyati River where I too have done some shooting, he agreed to act as a lookout on a kopje, one of the great piles of boulders that dot the southern bushveld, while some of his Boer friends tracked a small herd of buffalo bulls into some dense vegetation below. Reaching the top, Daly sat down to see what would happen and, after a few minutes, saw one of the hunters come out of the morass of bush into more open stuff. Surprised, Daly watched a buffalo carefully stalking the man from behind, approaching quietly and stealthily. Realizing that the buff was closing in to charge, Daly fired from the kopje and hit it in the shoulder. The astonished Afrikaaner spun around and saw the buff, finishing it off.

The experience earlier in this century of one Richard Berridge in what is now Tanzania typifies the chasing of buffalo around thick cover. Berridge wounded a buff at the edge of a swamp and it got into the reeds. An amateur, Berridge followed him up through dense cover only to find himself charged from behind; the bull had probably let the man go by and then boiled out of the bush in a deferred ambush. As Berridge spun around, he was badly laid open by a horn slash and completely knocked flat. The bull turned and charged again, hooking the man in a lovely arc over its head to land in a pile to the rear.

One admirable aspect of the buffalo is its persistence. Not especially pleased with its previous work, this buff came back a third time and now hooked Berridge through the ribs, breaking five and sticking a tent-peg–size hole in his lung.

Just as well that Berridge was now unconscious. The bull came back again and knelt on the bleeding man's chest so hard that a big, bloody-pink bubble of lung was forced out through the horn hole like an inflated wad of bubble gum. It then began to lick Berridge's face.

There has been a lot of pulp written about the buffalo's using its tongue and teeth as weapons. I have no personal knowledge of this rasping away of flesh with the tongue, which, if used for that purpose, would surely do the job as well as the finest tempered steel. Still, the report on Berridge is quite detailed and I'm not prepared to say that the buff didn't tear away as much of the skin of Berridge's face as his safari blacks said it did. Some writers maintain that the tongue is used on open wounds because of the buff's love of the salt in the blood, but that simply doesn't seem reasonable to me, although it may in fact be true. What animal would be thinking of its appetite when goring somebody to death? I honestly just don't know nor have I ever spoken to anybody in modern times who can give evidence of a similar case. I will, however, accept that Berridge's face was badly rasped.

Berridge was more than lucky. Just as it seemed that he was about to undergo some hoof therapy, the buffalo dropped dead. He was not only lucky but tough, for although his medical supplies were pretty well depleted and he was completely out of antiseptics, Berridge lived through the ten-day round trip it took to bring a doctor to him. He was eventually shipped home to England, but whether he made it or not is a piece of information that was not revealed by my research.

The power of a bull buff's toss is fairly incredible. Some eight years ago, I had the pleasure of interviewing my old friend, the late Berry Boswell Brooks, who was inducted in 1973 into the Hunting Hall of Fame, the first American to receive that honor. A grand old boy who had won the Weatherby Trophy as International Sportsman of the Year in 1959, Berry—who also funded his own branch of a museum in Memphis, Tennessee, called the Pink Palace—had been chosen by *Sports Afield* magazine in 1963 as one of the world's six greatest living hunters. He had also garnered the Allwyn Cooper Trophy for the best head of Indian game as well as the Nyalaland (a hunting area in Mozambique) Trophy for the finest head to come out of Mozambique.

I spent three days at Berry's home in Memphis, reminiscing with him and his wife about some of his safaris. Of course, the subject came around to buffalo, which comprised some of the 160 record-class trophies he had put into Rowland Ward's book. I taped the story of Roy Lintey, the late professional hunter who was killed by a buff the same day Berry just missed meeting him.

Don Ker and I had been out for three months and were hunting lion and buffalo in the Masai region. One morning a young *moran*—a "warrior"— came into camp to tell us there was another *m'zungu* or white man camped about ten miles away. Well, we were dying for someone to talk to and piled into the hunting car to go for a visit. When we arrived in the man's camp, the Swahili cook told us his *bwana* was off hunting with his *WaMericani* clients, but normally came back for breakfast about nine o'clock. As it was nearly that time, I took my binoculars and started to scan the plain for some sign of them and finally saw them coming from about a mile away. I told Don they were in sight and suggested we drive out to pick them up, but he opted for another cup of tea, not wanting to barge in on them.

As they got closer, I had the feeling something was wrong and could see through the binoculars that they were carrying something on a litter. I got Don going, and we drove the 'Rover out to see what was going on. As we got up to them I could see that it was a man they were carrying and I had trouble recognizing Roy Lintey, an independent professional hunter I had met two years before in Nairobi. His whole face had been crushed and literally pushed up to the top of the head. He was still conscious, but in terrible pain, and couldn't speak with his smashed jaw and cheekbones.

I always carry a first aid kit when I'm on safari and fortunately had several Syrettes of morphine in it. We gave him a couple and decided the best thing was to leave his clients in camp and try to get Lintey to the Game Department in Narok,

50

some fifty miles away. Don got on the radio to the late Lynn Temple- Borham, who was in charge there, and had him radio for a plane. On the way to Narok, I got the story from Lintey's gunbearer, who had witnessed the accident from a tree.

The client had wounded a big buffalo bull through the guts and it ran into a 5-acre tract of very heavy bush. True to his profession, Lintey told the client to wait on the other side of the tangle while he went in to root out the injured buff. Sending his trackers and gunbearers up trees to try to spot the bull, Lintey entered the cover alone with his .500/.465. He hadn't gone fifty feet when one of the men spotted the bull sneaking up on him and shouted a warning, whereupon the buffalo immediately charged. In the very thick bush, Lintey couldn't see the animal until it was almost on him, but courageously held his fire until sure of a killing shot. He made it, too, shooting the bull squarely between the eyes with the .500/.465, completely destroying the brain. But it was too late. Dead on its feet, the buffalo smashed into Lintey's stomach and then, almost as a reflex, wrenched his head up, catching Lintey full in the face with the boss of his horns.

The official report stated that Lintey died on board the aircraft from Narok, but I believe he was mostly gone at the time we loaded him on. Things like that kind of get you to thinking . . .

Most of the men who spend large chunks of the calendar in Africa as either professionals or amateurs have scary and true tales of the Cape buffalo. In fact, somebody once asked me at a National Rifle Association Convention why it was that so many people who had hunted there had "horror stories" about the buffalo, but that none of these hunters was dead. From the viewpoint of the reader, that's not an inappropriate inquiry.

The reason is that if you have been killed by a buffalo, you are unlikely to write about it later.

Actually, most of the really great buff stories are lost forever, for many of the hunters who experienced them and lived didn't have a literary bent. Professional hunters are not generally—and I use the term in knowledgeable exclusion of several pro friends—the book- or story-writing type, whatever that indicates. Nonetheless, hunters of the Cape buff have left us a sufficiently sanguinary legacy to preclude anybody's calling him a pantywaist.

John Hunter, previously mentioned as a bulwark of the *bwana* business, had an especially large number of exercises in heightened blood pressure with buff, although he was better known for his exploits with elephant and rhino. It was Hunter, in a book written in collaboration with Dan Mannix (for years my favorite writer for his monthly contribution to the old *True* magazine, which I read as a kid) who may have recorded some of the more exotic techniques used by attacking buffalo. Biting is one of them.

Hunter recorded the case of an Ndorobo tribesman, the original *shenzi* or "wild people" of Kenya, who had been charged by an *Mbogo* of determinate poor humor. On his way home on a tiny path, the Ndorobo jumped for his life as the buffalo poured down on him, just catching a low branch of a substantial tree. Apparently, the man and the buff looked at each other for a while until the black got a severe cramp in his right leg. I know that Africans hunker by the hour in

52

the most cramping positions imaginable to an *m'zungu*, or "white man," but this chap decided to put his foot down to stretch. Damned if I know, guys; you'd think he'd have found someplace more convenient to stretch it than in front of the buff's nose. Anyway, he did. In a flicker, the bull bit him, severing the heel from his foot. Somehow satisfied, the buff wandered off to wherever it is that satiated buff go, leaving the Ndorobo with a missing heel, producing the limp that prompted the recording of the story by Hunter.

Hunter cited zebra as typically severe biters and I wholeheartedly agree, but the buff is a bovine with teeth only in the bottom of the jaw and a fleshy pad above, hardly approved shearing equipment, although the power of the jaws can't be denied. Still, it'll be a long, long time before I suggest that J. A. Hunter was frivolous in his reporting.

Another rather macabre reflection by Hunter resulted from his considering the employment of a native game scout. Noticing some odd scars on the insides of the black's thighs, the *bwana* casually asked the man the cause. As is the way with the completely offhand bushfolk, the applicant dropped his loincloth to reveal that he had been well and truly neutered. As he explained to J.A., he had been passing through high grass while on the way to check over his artificial beehives, chunks of hollowed-out logs hung by bark fiber that bees, as well as snakes and birds, used to nest. Caught cold, a charging bull buff nailed him between the legs, pitching him into the air from whence he happened to fall straddled over the buffalo's back. Completely terrified, the black grabbed an ear with one hand and flattened the other against the huge shoulder for balance. Hunter said that the buff tore along with the man for sixty yards until he was knocked off, nearly unconscious, by a thornbush.

The last thing the man remembered was the charcoal gray and ebony horn of the hurtling buffalo as it hooked at his groin. The horn punched in, ripping flesh, sinew, and nerves. The African passed out.

The constitution and recuperative powers of the bush African are amazing by white standards, but the ordeal of the Ndorobo stands out even in a land where nature is not given to mollycoddling. It was almost dark when the man came to, in shock and unable to stand. In the last light, he realized that he had been flung near the bank of a small river and somehow agonizingly pulled himself over to the edge. One hand was crushed and broken, but he was able to scoop a little water with the other to ease his awful thirst. Feeling a bit better, he bathed his wounds.

Unbelievable as it may seem, the honey gatherer lay by the side of the stream for two weeks, still unable to move, staying alive by eating what grass he could reach. Lions never found him, nor did the hyenas, which would have almost certainly eaten him in his helpless condition. Both rhino and elephant came down to drink nearby but left him alone. Even crocs surfaced near him several times and stared but did not attack. Then, on a day when he had long been given up as dead by his village, another group of honey gatherers stumbled on him and took him home. Although his wounds had almost healed under the cool water, he was nearly dead of hunger. Hunter, fascinated by the man's obviously true story, couldn't understand why the black would want a job that would bring him back into contact with buffalo. J.A. quoted the man's answer: "Bwana, I will know that buffalo again by his horns. When I find him, I will cut off his *makende* and eat them, just as surely as he galloped off with mine."

Speaking of buffalo injuries that were survived, the journals of the Honorable William H. Drummond, which deal with hunting in southern Africa during the 1870s, offer a couple of beauties.

An African named Untabine who worked as chief hunter for Drummond's friend David Leslie had wounded a buffalo and was following it up in heavy cover. Sneaking down a narrow path lined with cactus plants, he heard that old grunt and spun around to find a cow buffalo right on top of him. He turned to run but was instantly gored, a terrific wound from a thick horn that slammed between the shoulder blades and passed completely through the body to emerge from just under the right breast.

Leslie, who saw the incident because he was on a straight part of the path, killed the buffalo with a lucky heart shot but saw little hope for Untabine, who was unconscious and whose lung hung largely out of the chest hole. Still, Leslie decided to try his best for his old friend and servant. He stuffed the lung back the way it had come and then used long camel thorns to skewer the edges of the wounds closed until they could be sewn up when the man was carried back to camp. Everybody sat around waiting for Untabine to die, but they were still waiting six months later when the man was back hunting buffalo! Incidentally, the cow buffalo proved to be unwounded.

Drummond also wrote of a Zulu who was famous among even his own people for the big game he had speared over the years, alone but for two or three dogs. Once when he was hunting buffalo, he crept close enough to a feeding herd to spear a bull with a thrown *assegai*. The animal covered about a mile before the dogs brought it to bay in a small clearing ringed with thornbushes. The Zulu worked in close for another throw, but the buffalo spotted him and, ignoring the dogs, charged.

The man cocked his arm and threw, hitting the buff but not slowing it, and the Zulu turned to run for a tree. He had just reached the nearest and started to climb when his foot slipped and the furious bull gored him in the thigh. Knocked free by another swipe of the horns that stabbed into his side, the man was thrown up and forward into a thorn tree, where a broken spike of dead branch lanced into the horn hole in his leg and held him crucified upside down for several horrible, painful minutes.

Fortunately, as the Zulu struggled to pull free, the buffalo followed the dogs a short distance off and lost sight of the man. At last, the flesh tore and the Zulu fell to the ground, crawling as quickly as he could to a hiding place under a thick shrub nearby. For some time the buffalo searched the area for his tormentor, coming quite close, but was unable to locate him. At last, it went away.

The Zulu was in bad shape, his thigh ripped terribly and his intestines protruding from the huge tear in his side. He was some nine miles from the nearest village and at least twelve miles from home, but he gritted his teeth and withdrew several of the very long *Umgokolo* thorns that were part of the daily headdress of the Zulus. Ignoring the pain, he pushed his guts back in and drove the steely thorns through the flesh on either side of his wound and fastened the sides together; he then managed to get his belt off and around his leg to staunch the bleeding. Then he began to walk.

Fainting from pain and loss of blood, resting frequently for an hour or two, and losing unknown time in half-coma, he never knew how long it took him until, more dead than alive, he saw a beehive Zulu hut, one of several. By sheer luck, it happened to be the *kraal* of which his uncle was *Umnumzana,* head of a group of huts. Had it been otherwise, he might have been denied admittance for fear that he would die and tribal complications arise.

Despite the severity of his wounds, the Zulu spear-hunter recovered, although long after the incident. Drummond wrote that the thigh still had a hole big enough for the white man to put his fist into, and the scar from the side wound was as big as a dessert plate.

There are surely many hundreds if not thousands of recorded buffalo encounters that have totaled up to a lot more than hangnails, neuralgia, and shinsplints, and they seem to have a lot of general factors in common. The most consistent element is that the buff has been wounded, either by the hunter or by a secondary agency. The second is that once he's in gear, it's mighty tough to get a buff back into neutral. Still, of all the fascinating material I've researched for this book, there are a couple of incidents that stick in my mind as downright interesting.

I really *like* primitive weapons and have twice spear-hunted buffalo, and have also been involved in trying to stick wild boar and other such activities generated by an unupholstered brain. Yet I think that the story recorded by the old Kenya hand Blayney Percival (not to be confused with Philip Percival) of a native hunter taking on a buffalo with his bush knife is one of the better I have read.

The African's name is not known, only that he used to sit up at night at a water hole near the Tana River, where historically much of Kenya's best ivory was taken. On one of his vigils, a herd of buffalo came in to drink, and the hunter wounded a bull with his old muzzle loader. Appreciating the better part of valor, he waited until the morning to follow it up.

The buff, hard hit but certainly not incapacitated, had entered a patch of vegetative bad news, fish-hooking around on his spoor so that he lay waiting on his own trail. Whether buff do this through cunning or merely to get the wind better is a matter of conjecture to this day, but many hunters following a wounded *Mbogo* are taken from behind after they pass the animal. I personally doubt that this is done purposely, but you're equally dead whether it is or it isn't.

Cramped and tired, the native hunter was on the spoor as soon as the sun was high enough to see the track, his musket recharged with a fresh lead ball. Startled as the buffalo broke cover and swarmed upon him, he fired apparently without effect, getting a horn completely through his upper leg.

Perhaps the shot had some effect after all. Instead of tossing the man away and tearing the muscle free from his thigh, the bull just walked along with the badly injured African hanging upside down from the horn, the hole in his leg as big as a cantaloupe. Probably because this didn't feel very good, the hunter reached up and found his knife in his belt, pulled it out, and began some *en route* surgery. As he repeatedly stabbed and slashed at the bull's throat, the blood began to pour down until the buffalo fell over with a convulsive shudder after tossing the man clear.

Percival certainly had no reason to question the veracity of the story, matching up the description with the big scars on both sides of the man's thigh. I reckon that the buff was about to cash in, barely under its own power after the long wait from the time it was wounded until it had a chance to place the hunter *en brochette*. Whatever, it is the only case I have found of a man killing a buffalo with a sheath knife.

As might well be understood, a man's own personal experiences with any animal are those most indelibly branded on his brain. One I will never forget happened in Zambia some years ago.

As corpses go, it was a real humdinger, the kind even a big-city coroner wouldn't forget in a hurry. It hung fifteen feet in the air above me, draped like a torn mannequin over the spiked branch of a yellow acacia. My thumb instinctively slipped onto the safety of the Evans .470 Nitro Express double rifle. Literally dead center, smack through the solar plexus, was a hole large enough to accommodate a fair-sized pumpkin if you shooed off the hundreds of iridescent green flies and maggots swarming over the torn mess. Two days of hanging in the searing sun and spring humidity had not rendered it especially beneficial to the general odor of the immediate area.

I started Invisible, my Number Two man, scraping away a shallow grave. Silent, my ancient, gnomelike Awiza gunbearer, cut a sapling and pushed the dead man from his grisly perch to land with a foul thump beneath the tree. The ground was mostly rockless, sandy clay, so we covered the grave with staked-down mounds of the meanest thorn bushes we could find to keep the hyenas and jackals from invading the poor man's privacy.

The spoor told the whole tale as clearly as a Dick and Jane primer. A mangled, smooth-bore muzzle loader lay fifty yards away, the fired percussion cap still pinched in place between the hammer and nipple. The wire-bound stock and barrel were ready for recycling, having been stamped into scrap. We easily retraced the big, splayed hoofprints to a shadowy stand of thick *mopane* where the two old Cape buffalo bulls had stood, dozing away the afternoon heat. The splintered end of a sap-oozing twig showed that the bullet had clipped it before slamming into meat—too far back, by the look of the dried blood. Probably guts or stomach. The wounded bull had immediately charged, while the second had run off a few yards and stood, confused. The hunter, a Senga tribesman whose name we later learned was Fantastic, had dropped the gun and run for the shelter of the big tree. He was still ten feet short when the bull smashed into him, shoving what was probably the right horn completely through the man's chest, back to front. The unbelievable power of the charge's impact had, by the look of the wound's diameter, pushed the horn clear up to the base. Then the toss had thrown him free, straight up to where he happened to land across a branch, probably already dead of a crushed spine.

The buff had then stopped, probably perplexed that the man was no longer in sight. For what must have been several minutes, he charged here and there before he smelled or saw the blood leaking down and spotted the body. From a point some four feet above the trampled ground, the bark had been bludgeoned and torn from the tree where the bull charged it, repeatedly trying to knock the man free. But the cruel thorns held the dead man, and the bull gave up, returning to the dropped gun, which he proceeded to pulverize until wandering off with his pal to nurse the terrible pain in his guts.

It was now my job to track him down, root him out of the thick stuff, and stamp him "Canceled." As Game and Elephant Control Officer of the district, it was my responsibility to kill him before he bumped into some poor beggar and put on his act again.

At first light the next morning, we break camp and immediately make for the Lundazi River on foot. As is my custom, I carry the .470 myself at any time visibility is less than one hundred yards. Silent tracks ahead, looking for spoor, while I cover him by watching the sides and far front. Invisible, just behind me, carries the water bag, my extra cartridges, and iron ration provisions for at least one night in case we have to sleep on the trail.

After about an hour of hunting, we cut what is surely the spoor of a pair of bulls leading from the water's edge and then back at a lazy angle into the heavy bush. I very much wish that somebody would come up with a more appropriate term than "heavy bush" that I could plagiarize. It simply does not fairly describe the morass of almost solid vegetative growth that lines the Lundazi to a depth of three hundred yards from its banks. Visibility is not measured in yards, but often in inches.

My tracker has found a lovely pile of near-steaming pasture patty that is not even glazed over. I stick my finger into it and discover that it is not fifteen minutes old. It also contains, I note with no little interest, large, dark clots of blood mixed in with the fecal material. Guess who.

We follow the spoor for another forty yards until a very convenient, thigh-thick sapling appears. As I cover the bush ahead, Silent, who is well named, sneaks noiselessly up the trunk until he is twenty feet above the tops of the surrounding ground cover. An errant swirl of wind doesn't do much for my confidence as I steal a glance up at him. He's staring hard at something, obviously indistinct, about fifty yards off. It seems like two weeks before he points with his chin and holds out two fingers, then a single finger up and another down. One bull is standing, the other lying down. Pointing out a direction, he looks expectantly down at me. Go get 'em, boy. Oh me, oh my. Silent, who is not stupid, will stay in the tree where I can see him, giving signals if the buffalo move. Like straight at me.

Following the azimuth he has indicated, I snick the safety off the Evans and begin creeping forward, picking each step in slow motion, walking on the outside edges of my sockless desert boots. After ten yards, I look back at Silent, who simply nods. Still there. Ahead, there is nothing but the shadowy tangles of branches, leaves, and grass woven more densely than an oriental rug. Every few yards I lie flat, trying to pick out the silhouette of a leg or the movement of a flicked tail or ear. Nope. You'd think that a couple of critters that push a ton or so would at least crack a twig or swish a leaf, maybe even break wind or something. Not bloody likely. I pause for a moment to persuade my heart to stop pounding so loud that I couldn't hear an express train if it were coming right at me. Fear and raw nerves are making me sweat, and my legs feel like spaghetti. Face it. I'm not scared, I'm terrified motherless.

Then an astonishingly familiar bovine odor smacks me in the face. And I realize I can hear the flies. I freeze into an idiotic statue, one foot off the ground. When you can smell them and even hear the flies, you have a fair hunch they're not awfully far away. My sweat-stung eyes probe every inch of alternating light and shadow ahead and to the sides as I try to lower my leg without losing my balance. That would be cute! A step. Another. Where are they? You want to shoot them, not take them prisoner!

Then, it's there, its very size making it nearly invisible in the dappled play of sun. But what is it? Well, I reason, if it smells like a Cape buffalo, makes tracks and droppings like one, draws flies and has a big slab of grayish-black hide with sparse bristles near enough to count, then it is fairly reasonable to assume that it *is* a Cape buffalo. Or, at the very least, *part* of a Cape buffalo. But which part and which one? I don't want to cash in the unwounded one unless I have to. Long, very long seconds creak and crawl by as I strain to figure out what I am looking at and whether it's the end that bites. Maybe just another few steps closer. At six yards—African yards are much shorter than the ones used to measure American football fields—your brain slips into panic overdrive. From between two leaves, a single, baleful eye is staring right at the center of your stomach. That's all, boys. I don't get paid *that* much. At eighteen feet, I couldn't give a howl in hell which bull it is. Hopefully, he doesn't yet realize what he's looking at either, so now's my chance. With the sneakiest possible movement, I level the Evans. The ivory bead mates with the vee of the single express rear leaf: Hold slightly over the eye and squeeze off.

The muzzle blast smothers any sound of bullet strike, and for an incredible millisecond, there is silence. It is, however, a mini-millisecond because now the air is alive with shouts from Silent, very unsociable grunts from a couple of feet away, and the noise of the radical redecoration of some local flora. The second bull, whichever one he is, has unquestionably had his attention gotten and is charging, bearing down invisibly through the heavy bush with an irresistible power that is hair-raisingly awesome. I jump a few yards to my left as he breaks cover, exactly where I was standing, attacking the sound of the hated gun. He is clearly not very happy with me.

The reflex that has kept me alive through all these uninsurable years in a never exactly dull business has the .470 doing its little act all by itself. As he swings toward you—head high, changing direction—a charming, white-edged hole appears between his eyes, right at the base of his big, black, wet nose. He's hardly hit the ground, blood pouring from his ears, before the Evans is broken and new rounds chambered. Another solid throws a puff of dust from the back of his neck. Sure he's down for the count, I spin and level the rifle back at the place where that spooky eye was, holding it in its marvelous balance by the pistol grip, index finger on the second trigger while I fish out another cigar-sized cartridge from my pocket with my left hand and reload the fired chamber.

I need not have bothered. The first bull is lying where he dropped, the solid slug neatly through his left eye as he looked at me. He's as dead as my innocence and the tax shelter combined, but even though .470 Kynochs are worth their weight in sterling silver, I stick to the rule that's kept me ambulatory and swat him in the nape of the neck anyway.

The urge for a cigarette and a long, absolutely obscene scotch are overwhelming as I sit down ten yards away. I manage the cigarette on the third try, just as Silent and Invisible come up, wholesaling the usual *eeeeehhhs* and *aaaaahhhhs* of the excited bush African. When we roll over the bulls as the fat red ticks begin to drop off the crotch area, sensing death, we are able to determine that it was the second bull that had been wounded. Silent digs out a wicked chunk of iron-reinforcing rod that had passed through five coils of intestine and lodged against the far skin's inside. A couple of feet forward, and it would have been a fine lung shot and the late, lamented Fantastic would have been the village hero.

By the time we have taken the interior fillets and the tails to turn in to the government, the circle of human vultures had moved in. They had likely been following us from the village all day, waiting for the sound of my shots. When we finish the walk back to the 'Rover, I take a healthy belt of scotch, grill some of the fillets, and spend the rest of the day driving back to base camp. I certainly haven't enjoyed the business of following up somebody else's wounded buffalo, I reflect as the hunting car rocks and scrapes along the light bush track, but it sure as hell beats the real fight for survival back in civilization.

3 RHINO

THE TOWERING ZAMBIAN SUN is hot, yet the shadows are refreshingly cool in the low humidity of the July winter as you walk slowly behind Silent, the grass swishing softly against your bare legs. Ahead, within easy reach, bounces the buttstock of the Evans .470 Nitro Express double rifle, carried by the barrels over Silent's shoulder. The worn pink rubber of the recoil pad seems somehow an insane choice for a masterpiece of Circassian walnut and soft scrolling. You wonder idly if years back there was an overrun on soles for Pat Boone's white bucks that found its way to London. From time to time, you flick a small leafy branch at the old man's back to shoo the tsetse flies that alight there and feel the same fluttering motion as Invisible clears your shoulders of the sneaky little bloodsuckers. You have long gotten used to the whine of the stingless *mopane* bees mobbing your face to drink the moisture of your sweat. A glance at the next dung pile shows that the buffalo herd is only a half-hour ahead, and you know that at this hot time of the day they won't be moving fast. Any minute now you should spot the tail of the herd and pick out a fat young bull for staff rations.

No word or sign is necessary. As the thought crosses your mind, Silent is already passing the rifle and dropping back. You need not follow the track any longer; visual contact is imminent. Considering the size of the herd, you decide to swap the 500-grain solid bullet in the right barrel for a soft-point to minimize the chance of the big slug's passing through your target animal and wounding another beyond him. You'll keep the cupro-nickel–jacketed solid in the left barrel just in case a rear raking shot is called for or a charge must be stopped. Another pair of solids are between the fingers of your left hand where they always are, so familiar that you have eaten an entire sandwich without realizing that they were still stuck there.

Let's see, now, you pull out the little binoculars from the breast pocket of your department-issue tunic and start scanning the dense tangles of bush ahead. Nothing yet. The wind's fine though, medium and steady into your face as you move quietly off to the right to clear a dense stand of dry, shade-haunted *tshani* grass. After another two hundred yards and many pauses to glance ahead, the whip of a tail at last is telegraphed through the dusty lenses, and other patches of dark, sparsely bristled hide stand out through the few gaps in the cover. They're about a hundred yards off, feeding slowly along in a low reddish haze like ground fog raised by hundreds of hooves against the dry earth.

Leaving your men where they are, you begin to slip forward and stalk the herd, looking for a likely candidate for the Big Surprise. At forty yards, you edge up to a big tree and look the lot over again. Lord, but there's a slather of them! Some hulking, scarred bulls with worn horntips and heavy, corrugated helmets of boss are off to one side. Unusual, as they are not often found with the women and kids. Cows, some with calves at heel, are scattered all about and—oh, yes— there you are. A trio of 1,200-pounders begins to wander by at an angle directly in front of you, only thirty yards away. You ease the Evans up and into a careful rest over your thumb while your hand presses steadily into the side of the tree. It's as solid as a bench rest, a perfect setup for a nice, neat spine shot that will drop him instantly so that he won't get the adrenaline up and make next week's dinners taste like cutlets carved from a boiled, steel-belted radial. The fine, blackened bead of the foresight nestles into the shallow wedge of the rear as you start your squeeze on a spot a third of the way down from the top of his shoulder. But you never complete it . . .

A chorus of warning yells erupts from behind you, and at the same instant the buffalo herd explodes into a panicked stampede, only a few animals visible through the choking pallor of dust and churning dirt. Confused, you swing around, so startled that your first reaction is anger. Not for long. Among the dashing, yelling men, a dark rushing form appears, and the weird *chuff-chuff* of a furious rhino is loud even over the thunder of the running buffalo.

Bloody hell! A thunderbolt of panic tearing through you, you watch helplessly as the rhino closes in on Invisible as if he were standing still. Headed right at you, the man's body shields the rhino until, just as he realizes he is about to be caught, he throws himself off to one side. With unbelievable grace for his two tons of muscle, the bull hauls up with the delicacy of a polo pony, reverses direction, and is on Invisible before he can roll away. It all seems to happen in slow motion, the lowering of the great spiked head, the burst of dirt and leaves, and the awful sight of Invisible with his arms wrapped around the rhino's head and face as tightly as he can hang on.

With the African still clutching the animal for dear life, the rhino snorts and starts to run off. With as careful an aim as a quick shot permits, you slam the soft-point into the center of the shoulder, the .470 blowing a puff of dried dirt from the heavy skin. A torrent of blood erupts from the bull's nostrils as it tosses, and Invisible arches through the air to land in a tangled heap twenty-five feet away. While he is still airborne, you stick the second bullet into the juncture of rhino neck and body. The rhino collapses as if electrocuted. Reloading, you shoot it again and reach Invisible just as Silent does. Anguish and despair swirl through you when you see him covered with blood and lying on his face, and he is cautiously rolled over. Incredibly, there is no horn hole; the blood is mostly that of the rhino, which has soaked Invisible when the lung shot apparently also caught a big artery.

A far more literary type than you once observed that true happiness is the sudden, unexpected cessation of unbearable pain. Maybe. Whatever it is, it isn't far from your relief on seeing your faithful old companion's eyes open and come into focus. Gasping for breath, he lies there for a few minutes, feeling for broken bones, and then climbs painfully to his feet. Both you and Silent are half-hysterical that he is unhurt, let alone still alive, and the mood changes to lunatic good humor. Silent reminds him that he, Invisible, owes him money. You threaten to run him in for attempted rhino poaching and suggest that if he plans to take it up as a profession, he'd better quit trying to catch them with his bare hands.

Over cigarettes and water, you listen to Invisible describe his feelings as the big bull trundled over and stuck its front horn into the dirt six inches in front of the man's stomach. By reflex, he could think of nothing else to do but grab the horned head and hang on to keep from being gored. Certainly, if he hadn't, he would have gotten a very impressive new navel. As the relieved laughter and joking die down and smokes are relit, you can see Silent and Invisible glancing back and forth at each other. Something is afoot, for sure.

"Nyalubwe," ventured Silent in Fanagalo, calling me by my African name, "what do you suppose happened to that *uBejane* over there that he is dead?" I looked at him, puzzled as they both made the classic African gesture of surprised amusement of covering their mouths with their hands.

When I didn't answer, Invisible picked it up. "What *uBejane* is that, Silent?" he innocently asked, looking around. "Ahhh. I see it now! Let us go and look, then come and advise Nyalubwe of the wounds."

They rose and walked carefully around the carcass, hands behind their backs, frowning in concentration. Walking back over to me, Silent rested his chin in his hand with great seriousness.

"*Tagati,* Bwana," he said sagely. "It must have been black magic. Or maybe lightning. There is no mark of arrow or spear upon him, and we have both most carefully inspected him."

"Bwana," chimed in Invisible, "might it not have been too much time with his wives? It is that time of year. Too much time spent with women can kill a man. Why not a rhino? Yes, I believe it was that."

Finally, it dawned on me what they were trying to do. In Zambia, the killing of a rhino even in self-defense is a very serious offense, the perpetrator of which is usually presumed to be guilty until, rarely, proven innocent. They were trying to protect me from the prosecution I probably would have received if I had still been a professional hunter working for the safari company instead of a Game Control Officer. Being a bit hazy on the logic of the mysterious workings of the game department, they were offering to back me up in a false report that the rhino had been found dead and had not been shot by me. I could have explained to them that it was no problem, but then they would have been cheated out of their gesture of loyalty, a loss of face even among such good friends as we.

"Hmmmm," I pondered out loud. "It may be that you elders are right. In any case, let us cut out the interior fillets and all the better meat we can carry as well as the horns for the government. We shall drink a little beer at camp to give us strength and speak more of this matter before I send the paper-that-speaks along with the horns."

With sly grins, they set to work with their hatchets and knives, certain that they had saved me from a fate worse than sobriety. Back at camp, I sent the horns off to headquarters along with my report, telling the truth of the incident. After all, I was the chap in charge of the area, and if I called it self-defense, who was to gainsay me? I was and still am certain that had I not killed the rhino, it would have gotten Invisible. As it was, nothing less than a miracle was responsible for his survival despite my somewhat tardy action.

Zambia is one of the last great strongholds of the black rhino, by far the most dangerous of the two African species. Although substantial numbers of black rhino live in the *miombo* tree scrub of Zambia's Luangwa Valley, the safari company that controlled

the shooting concessions at the time of Invisible's encounter was permitted only five rhinos per year for its
clients, and those at extremely high license fees. So,
because of the substantial foreign exchange each animal represented, woe to any poor white hunter forced
to kill a rhino in self-defense or for any other con-
ceivable reason off license. Thus, in the old safari
days, our time was far better spent in trying *not* to find
rhinos than hunting them.

The willingness of a rhino to charge just about anybody or anything is due to three factors: poor eyesight, great curiosity, and a fabulously advanced state
of stupidity. As is typical, we had done nothing to try
to bother the bull who wanted to place Invisible *en
brochette* just in the name of good, clean fun; good
gravy, we didn't even know he was there! When we
moved crosswind, stalking the buffalo, our scent blew
into that patch of grass we had swerved to avoid. Old
uBejane caught it and just came boiling out for some
jollies. The next one might have run for his life in the
other direction. With all dangerous big game, you
never know. With the rhino, I doubt even *he* knows.

I owe my phenomenal skill at steeplechase running
and tree climbing largely to the black rhino. With typical modesty, I advise you that I have twice won the
Central African Invitational as well as having accumulated case lots of loving cups for Advanced Rhino
Avoidance and Active Applied Cowardice (Rhino Division). I am, to be further candid, something of a legend in my own time. My fame for attracting angry
rhinos the way a nudist colony draws mosquitos is still
spoken of throughout Africa in hushed, reverent whis-
pers. I never knew what it was; maybe just bad breath
or the heartbreak of psoriasis, but if you were to line
up a hundred people and turn loose one irate rhino (as

if there was any other kind), I would lay you very good odds that he would pick Very Sincerely Yours as his target. I have probably spent more time swaying in treetops than the average baboon and have certainly run as many miles trying to cut the wind on angry rhinos who just suspected that I was around as I have chasing poachers. Where rhinos are concerned, there's just *something* about me, and I doubt it's my winning smile. Yet, to show you how much I deserve all those awards, over the years I only once have actually had to kill a rhino, the bull who carried off Invisible. But sometimes it was very, very close.

One of the oddest incidents involving a rhino happened to a pal of mine, a fellow professional hunter back when I was doing sport safaris with clients. It seemed pretty funny later, known as "the day when Jack got bagged," but was no joke at the time. He was out with a single client on "fly" camp, following elephant spoor with a couple of his men and a pair of light tents. As he tells it, dawn was just coming up, and he was about to crawl out of his sleeping bag. All of a sudden things got a bit confused as a rhino took some sort of dislike to his tent and charged it. Of course, the horns snarled in the canvas and ropes, and the *uBejane* took off through the bush, blinded by the cloth, which was now a huge sack containing my friend. He took one hell of a battering over the 150 yards the rhino dragged him but luckily was not stepped on or gored. Maybe the sleeping bag cushioned him from some of the concussion of being slammed against trees and anthills, but not much. When the rhino finally shed the tent and pranced off, Jack looked as if he'd fallen into an active, empty cement mixer.

My own hairy occasions with rhinos have sometimes

required a good deal of bluff, not a tactic that leaves one with any particular feeling of security, as the odds are dead even that the rhino *isn't* bluffing. As a rule of thumb, provided that the individual circumstances of the confrontation make such a move practical, the best way to avoid trouble—besides staying home—is to climb a tree or otherwise put yourself out of reach. I do not recommend fragile trees. At close quarters, tree climbing likely won't be possible, and any attempt to run when a rhino is clearly bearing down carries a high instance of fatality.

Like all the big stuff, rhinos are amazingly fast, and despite what some have written, are nearly impossible to dodge for any length of time. Many weathering tombstones will bear me out on this. Given a direct charge over reasonably open terrain (not forgetting that prayer couldn't *hurt*), a good shout and clapping and waving of the hands *may* turn a rhino. It may also make him charge faster since he can now see your motion more clearly. I have broken several charges with a shot into the ground between the forefeet or, failing that, a bullet into the horn. It doesn't always work but normally will cause an unwounded rhino to turn. Oddly, unlike buffalo and many elephant, rhino are fairly easily turned. This, in my personal opinion, places them at the bottom of the traditional list of dangerous big game, although they do kill a lot of people who, understandably, would not share my views.

uBejane—Zulu for "the vicious one"—would be considered most aptly appellated by a very large stack of people who have had fatal or nearly fatal differences of opinion with the black rhino. "Bwana" Cottar, the progenitor of a slather of prominent members of the Kenyan professional hunting fraternity, is a handy example. Cottar—saints preserve us—an

American from Oklahoma who on more than one occasion strangled leopards to death with his bare hands (personally, I would have used gloves), finally had his gong rung by a rhino who gored him neatly through the heart. Major Chauncey Hugh Stigand, my personal hero of the good old days in eastern Africa and a one-man chapter in *Death in the Silent Places,* got himself remodeled so badly by a rhino that his whole pectoral muscle system was ripped free of his rib cage. The imperturbable Chauncey, who was speared to death in 1919 by the Aliab Dinka tribe, sat down and waited to see if his lung was punctured, which would result in his drowning in his own blood. Happily, it wasn't, to the subsequent joy of a lioness who ate large portions of his right arm and an elephant who tusked him through a thigh, not to mention the Nilotic Dinkas themselves. The notable—if inept—hunter and railway builder working on the Kenya–Uganda "Lunatic Line," Colonel J. H. Patterson, who ultimately settled the hash of the Tsavo man-eating lions, recorded the trials of an associate named Eastwood who forgot to pay the insurance on a presumably dead *Kifaru,* as the rhino is known in East Africa. Eastwood was left with a set of ribs that looked like the leftovers of a Florida barbecue, a shattered arm, and a double tossing garnished with a hole in the thigh that would store a mailbox. Eastwood was lucky, though. Although his arm had to be taken off, the vultures that gathered to finish up the rhino's leavings attracted his camp staff and he actually survived.

A Dr. Kolb, a personal pal of Bror von Blixen-Finecke, who was quite well known around the turn of the century in German East Africa (now Tanzania) as both a scientist and hunter, didn't do quite so well while bird hunting one lovely afternoon. Kolb, armed with only a scatter-gun, heard the lone female rhino snorting through the bush as she bore down on him. Realizing that No. 6 birdshot was probably a bit light, he started running like hell just as the big cow burst out of the cover. Had he been thinking, he would have given her a faceful of pellets and probably blinded her. He was, however, not thinking. For several seconds there followed a game of ring-around-the-thornbush for keeps, the rhino right behind the doctor. On his last circuit, Kolb noticed a big tree with a large, presumably rotten cavity near the ground and jumped into the hole.

He shouldn't have done that.

The rhino spun back, stuck her long horn into the opening and unzipped Dr. Kolb from the proverbial to the sublime with a couple of slashes of her horn, bringing both the gentleman's career and carcass to distinguished, if messy, ends. His accompanying natives, watching from nearby trees, found the body in such bad shape that even with their cast-iron sensitivities some were sufficiently affected to have lost their breakfasts.

Speaking of natives, the pioneer of nature photography in East Africa, C. Schillings, mentioned a safari porter of his who was caught by a rhino while the safari was on the march. Although the man's guts were largely pulled out of his horn hole, he recovered "no worse for the experience." Lord, and to think of the Rolaids I have to use!

Rhinos are definitely screwy and not to be fooled with, but some of their escapades illustrate a potential for ground-zero–class destruction besides. Strong? Listen to this one:

It was during the building of the Mombasa-Victoria-Uganda Railway between Mombasa and Lake Victoria, and whereas rhinos not uncommonly charged large assortments of rolling stock, employees, and laborers, one instance recorded by Richard Tjader is extraordinary on any basis. A gang of coolies were fastening a rail to its sleepers or ties not far from the construction car, a movable office that followed the line along as it was built. A huge bull rhino made a dramatic appearance out of the nearby thornbush of the Tsavo region and scattered the workers like a lion among chickens. Presumably feeling shortchanged at not having caught any of the imported Indians, the bull turned his undivided attention to the construction car. Incredible as it may seem, in his efforts to disembowel the metal interloper on the tracks, he flipped the entire car over and off the rails! Seemingly satisfied, he jabbed the steel undercarriage a few more times and retired from the field of honor. The workmen had hell's own time getting the heavy railroad car back on the rails, despite their great numbers. That, I dare say, is *strong*.

On a more personal basis, Drummond left an account of a classic confrontation between rhino and man that dates all the way back to 1871 in Zululand. Considering the bravery and organization of the Zulu, who made, shall we say, a penetrating impression on British troops a few years later, the story is all the more remarkable.

As a short preface, the Zulu war machine was divided into the regimental system, all with revered names and titles that would be well understood by any British member of a similar regiment whose honor went back hundreds of years and over untold thousands of corpses. There's not all that much difference between *assegai* and bayonet, especially at places such as Rorke's Drift and Insandlwana.

Before bringing up the matter of the Zulu regiment and the rogue rhino, perhaps the observation that Zulu warriors did what they were bloody well told could be well illustrated by a passage in the recollections of William Finaughty. . . .

When Finaughty was twenty-one, in the year 1864, the great King Mzilikazi led the Matabele Zulu nation. Among the king's quirks was an affection for crocodiles, in whom he possibly saw a likeness. Finaughty reported that to kill one in Mzilikazi's kingdom was worth a man's life, but when a small child was taken by a very large *iNgwenya* ("the lawless criminal") and the local people complained, the king gave a simple command: "Bring them both to me."

By God, an entire regiment hopped to it! With incredible bravado, the warriors swarmed the river until they caught *by hand* the croc described as the child-eater and actually carried it unhurt into the king's presence accompanied by at least portions of the body of the dead child. Finaughty doesn't record the casualties involved, but if you don't think a croc is powerful, especially one described by an old bush hand as "an enormous fellow," you are terminally mistaken.

Finaughty wasn't present during Mzilikazi's "judgment" of the croc, but the impression of the thousand or more warriors carrying the helpless giant reptile and the pathetic toothtorn child to the royal *kraal* stayed with him his whole long life, which was last reported as having lasted well into its eighties.

In fact, if you've ever seen *Zulu*, the movie that launched Michael Caine, you may appreciate what Finaughty saw as the triumphant *impi,* or regiment, danced and sang its way into the royal presence, the staccato crash of spear butts on oxhide shields reverberating like thunder in their chests, the shrill ululations of the unmarried women quavering in waves of high, shattered sound over the huge expanse of the beehive hut capital. Son of a nevermind; if you don't have time for the amaZulu, you just don't know anything about fighting men!

So much for the croc. An interesting match, rogue rhino against two thousand seasoned Zulu warriors, wouldn't you think? It sure was. . . .

It was seven years later, in 1871. For some time, according to Drummond, a lone bull rhino had lived in a riverine thicket and had caught and killed at least three native women when they went to draw water. Of course, as was the way of the Zulu, the beast was considered to be well involved in supernatural matters, but nothing was done about the rogue until a son of the king died of natural causes and, consistent with custom, all the warriors of the various regiments were sent into the bush to hunt, the "washing" of their spears in blood being required to purify the nation from the supposed consequences of the death of the royal prince.

The regiment chosen to beard the behemoth in its lair was one of the most famous of the amaZulu (literally "the people of heaven"). Originally raised in 1854 under King Mpande, over the next two years it was incorporated into and had taken over the names of two additional regiments, the *isiBabule,* "sulphur," and the *iNkonkoni,* or "wildebeeste." The extended regiment was called by Drummond the *Tulwane* but is more properly known as the uThulwana, or "dust raisers." They were in the classic "loin" reserve when the British were annihilated at Insandlwana in January 1879 and one of the premier attack regiments at Rorke's Drift, so dear to the hearts and bloodshot eyes of late-night TV movie freaks such as Yours

Faithfully. They were one hell of a bunch of boys, I promise you, an honored regiment who disdained any footwear through the thorniest of country and who could—and bloody well did—fight and win battles after *running* fifty miles! There have been times I could have used a few of them. . . .

Thus, it was the uThulwana who were set in classic formation against a single killer bull rhino in the funereal hunt, their pure white shields, honorary badges of a well and often blooded old regiment, flashing in the sun like waves on a distant beach, while the fresh-whetted iron of their stabbing *assegais* glistened like two thousand wood and metal fangs. The chill of the August morning still lay about the naked ankles of the hunters beneath the black and white cowtail dangles tied below their knees as they advanced on the signal of their *indunas,* regimental colonels or leaders. The two thousand tried warriors, each wearing the headring granted by the king to signify the right to marry through valor, moved in a classic attack formation resembling a bull buffalo's horns, loins, and chest. A roar as mighty as a waterfall in spate washed over the dry winter air as the butts of their *ixwa,* stabbing spears named for the sucking sound they produced when pulled from an enemy's chest, slammed in unison into the rawhide of the tall shields. A tremendous war cry of *uSuthu!* seemed to whip up even more dust than the stamping naked feet as the *impi* approached and encircled the big thicket. Had it not been drowned by the shouts of the Zulu, another sound would have been audible: the chuffing of a charging bull rhino that was tearing through the bush directly toward the center of the regiment.

The rhino broke cover when the spearmen were within thirty yards of the thicket, three thousand or more pounds of horned determination. In a blur it was on the first rank, squarely hitting a veteran. As his shield was smashed away, the man thrust powerfully at the rhino's chest with his *ixwa*. Its dagger point penetrated only a few inches of thick hide, but the horn thrust home in a gout of crimson. The man sailed away to land in a heap, already dead from the great cavity in his chest. As other warriors hurled themselves on the raging rhino, it quickly spun and caught another man with its front horn, wrenching the spike deep and then powering on to crush him under pounding feet.

A blizzard of white ostrich feathers erupted from headdresses as the uThulwana warriors were smashed aside by the rushes of the bull rhino, now sprouting some *assegai* shafts from his barrel-stave ribs that had been shivered there by powerful black arms. (As was the Zulu fighting technique, the spears could not simply be thrust into the bull but had to be held in place and pushed deep with a shivering motion.) A full minute went by, then another, and the beaten grass at the edge of the thicket was dotted darkly with injured men. Still, the rhino snorted and charged into masses of Zulu, shouts of anger and pain cutting the dusty pall as the determined men tried to stand and stab the ever more determined *uBejane*. Another headringed fighter crawled off into the bush, the grayish-purple ropes of his intestines bulging between his fingers. He tried to stand, bracing himself against his blood-smeared shield, then fell dead.

Lung blood was now starting to ooze from the bull's nose and mouth from the growing bristle of *ixwa* sprouting from its thick hide. Still, despite the number and severity of its wounds, the rhino would not fall. It had killed three of the bravest warriors outright and was only starting to weaken when it caught a famous *induna,* a high officer of the *impi,* and killed him with a single toss, the limp body thumping and bouncing on the winter-hard ground in a tatter of genet tails, feathers, and leopard skin. At last, the rhino began to slow and the fighters swarmed in, screaming with bloodlust, stabbing insanely. Finally, carrying what Drummond reckoned as at least a thousand spears, the rhino fell, quivered, and died.

Tough animals, rhinos.

The object of this discussion is the so-called black rhino, but the color designation has nothing whatever to do with its actual hue. There are two African species of rhinoceros, the prehensile-lipped browser *Diceros bicornis,* or black rhino, and the square-mouthed grazer with the handle of *Ceratotherium simus.* He's the white rhino, a title as misleading as that used to designate his African cousin. All rhinos are, well, uh, rhino-colored. Not known for advanced standards of personal hygiene, they tend to be the color of the last thing they were rolling in. In East Africa's Tsavo country, for example, they're as pink as the local elephants from the rosy dust of the area, but in most places they're about the shade of a newly painted destroyer and not much less lethal.

Let's not get sidetracked by the square-lipped rhino, for although he has made an astonishing comeback as a species, he's not really a very menacing or challenging game animal. In fact, the records of Zululand, the territory of his southern range where he has traditionally been in greatest evidence, show that only four people have been clumsy enough to have gotten fatally in his way. He's the second largest of the land animals on earth but about as dangerous under unprovoked circumstances as a defanged Yorkshire terrier. The "white" bit comes from a misinterpretation by English-speaking hunters of the Dutch *wyd,* meaning wide or broad and not referring at all to the color of the beastie. Personally, I've never even seen a wild white rhino, although traditionally they occur in large numbers in two areas: South Africa and what used to be the Shangri-La of ivory poachers, the Lado Enclave of the Sudan. At one time, the species was reckoned to be down to seventeen animals—probably a severe underestimation—and even pronounced extinct, a *definite* underestimation of his numbers. Today, as we'll later see, the white rhino is actually *over*populating parts of his range, something you don't hear a great deal about from the self-styled preservationists.

Of course, there are other types of rhino, particularly in Asia, which features a triple billing of Sumatran, Javanese, and Indian varieties, but if you're a vertebrate zoologist, please don't write me any letters. Some have one horn, some two. All are smaller than the African twosome and look quite different, especially in the platelike formation of their heavy skin armor and a tendency toward being hairy. At least one is reported to prefer biting those who upset him to using the horn. Further, rhinos were all the rage in such unexpected places as North America not all that long ago, during the interglacial Pleistocene, which offered a very successful member of the club known as the woolly rhinoceros. He was a contemporary of the mammoth and like the proto-elephant has been found in assorted scraps frozen in ice. We do know that man, the emerging hunter, probably had the same experiences with him that we do today with his descendants. Personally, I'll take the .375 or the .470 over the club and the spear. . . .

It's almost interesting that the shortsighted stupidity of the black rhino can at times appear humorous, provided that you're not the person involved. In his 1909 book, *Land of the Lion,* W. S. Rainsford wrote of a missionary friend who, as a man of peace, took pride in always traveling unarmed. Usually, he would walk, but on longer journeys through the *nyika* would use a mule. He was on a mule during the incident described, riding through some very thick bush when he was suddenly charged by a rhino.

Consistent with the European terror of the African sun, the missionary, Mr. Shauffaker, was carrying a parasol at the time. The rhino devastated and killed the mule, barely allowing the missionary time to throw himself off before attacking him. It gave him a glancing blow, the horn thrusting past to take the main material of the parasol, leaving only the looped handle in Shauffaker's hand as the obviously pagan rhino made off through the bush. The missionary's last sight was the gay material of the sunshade disappearing in a cloud of dust.

Blayney Percival, appointed as game warden by the East African Protectorate (now Kenya), experienced a rhino attack at night, something I have had no personal exposure to. By the old books, rhinos are quite active after dark, especially during the hot season, and have often been known to drop by unsuspecting camps. Percival, who arose to a call of nature at about two in the morning, was wandering blearily around the campsite when a tremendous animal rushed past him, headed for the tent he had just left. An instant later, the blackness was shattered by a tearing crash as a bull rhino slammed into the canvas and wood supports. Unfortunately, there was another man in the tent when the rhino hit it. When the rhino had boiled off into the moonless night, the man in the tent emerged, covered with jam but unhurt through one of those minor miracles that lurk around African rhino incidents. His only question to Percival was, "Is it a tornado?"

The bed that Percival had left only a few seconds before was crushed into a lifetime supply of matchsticks, whereas the one in which his companion was sleeping was left untouched by the pounding feet. The rhino had stepped on a tin of strawberry jam, which, under its great weight, had exploded like a bomb, coating the man and everything in the tattered tent with the sweet, sticky stuff. It was bad luck that Percival's safari staff was in the same line of charge, for one black had been badly injured under the trampling feet and another clutched a nasty gouge that the rhino's horn had dug across his forehead.

Bror von Blixen-Finecke, an early Kenya professional hunter, wrote of a rhino that he and his friend Cooper encountered while stalking two lions. From the thick bush came the chuffing of an irate rhino that was almost on them before they could jump out of the way. Cooper didn't quite make it, and the rhino's horn caught under the strap around his neck from which his binoculars were suspended. The rhino tore off with Cooper in tow, but luckily the worn strap broke, or he surely would have had his neck broken. Blixen couldn't fire for fear of plugging his pal and figured that the man would have been killed if the strap had been new.

The multimillionaire Alfred Vanderbilt, a steady client of Blixen's, was also able to bring home an interesting rhino tale. The two were hunting guinea fowl and Blixen had just killed a brace with his light rifle, probably a .22, when his blacks shouted that a pair of rhinos were on their way. Bushwise, Blixen had his heavy rifle along, but it was being toted by the gunbearer, who was some distance away retrieving the guinea fowl. The two rhinos took after Vanderbilt and were almost on him when Blixen caught up with the gunbearer, grabbed his express rifle, and snapped a shot that instantly killed the lead rhino exactly six feet from Vanderbilt's tail. The second sheared off and disappeared into the bush.

Compared with the other heavyweights of The Big Five, rhinos are supposed to be fairly easy to kill despite their bulk. Yet, like any of the big boys, they can carry more lead than a shot tower when hit badly the first time around. An English friend of Richard Tjader was killed by a bull rhino after delivering twelve shots from a .500 Express, the hunter gored to death despite the extended fusillade. One immediately suspects just plain bum shooting, but Tjader's autopsy revealed that this was by no means the case. Two bullets struck the heart and certainly another two—perhaps three—had taken the lungs. Yet the rhino still wandered off for another hundred yards after killing the hunter.

One reads so much about it that I don't think it worth dwelling on the fact that rhino horn—not actually horn but the same material that fingernails are composed of—is prized as an aphrodisiac, especially in the East, and the high prices it commands have greatly contributed to the decline of the species where poaching is rampant. The "horn" isn't anchored to the skull bones at all but rests in a shallow socket supported by skin and what I guess would best be called gristle. This was well illustrated by Alan and Joan Root's "Balloon Safari," shown on educational TV. Finding a recently dead rhino, Alan gave the horns a few stout whacks with a hardwood stick from the side and pop! Off they came, intact. I don't think a trophy would be very well treated this way, but Root was collecting them for the government in any case.

The size of rhino horns can be astounding. The *Numero Uno* entry in Ward's Records is the 62¼-incher that came from the collection of the pioneer hunter Gordon-Cumming, taken from a white rhino. Cumming doesn't mention whether or not he actually killed it, which makes me think that he probably did not but traded with some native for it. Certainly, such an event would have been worthwhile for an author to record! No matter, five feet and change of rhino horn is incredible. The record black rhino horn is credited to the Tanzanian Game Department, which possesses a front horn measuring forty-seven and a quarter inches. In most cases, the horn of female rhino is longer than that of the male although as a rule much thinner in girth. "Gertie," a famous and often photographed Kenyan rhino cow, is a whopper, with a weird pigsticker that projects straight off her nose like a leveled lance.

Freak rhino horns aren't all that rare, for the individuals can vary widely in the shape of their horns. Almost surely a lot of the aberrant twists and turns result from injury in youth while the horn is still growing, thus influencing its later appearance and conformation. Although I don't recall where it was collected, we have a set of black rhino horns in the Explorers Club in New York City with the second horn overlapping and twining over the front one. C. R. S. Pitman, in his 1942 book, *A Game Warden Takes Stock,* mentions a three-horned black rhino from Uganda that resembles the rhino pictured in Blixen's book, opposite page 103, captioned as having been shot in 1932. It was probably the same rhino, for Blixen was a contemporary and friend of Pitman in Kenya. The "extra" horn is very small, rather palm-shaped, and located all the way up between the ears on the forehead. Pitman says that the third horn probably weighed about an ounce. Incidentally, although I doubt it influenced the growth of the third horn, the posterior or second horn of this rhino is badly bent downward so that the point ends in a loop below the shaft of the front horn. Perhaps it had its genes scrambled by some witch doctor.

Just how dangerous is the rhino? As with any of the other species that kill people, it always depends upon the experiences of the individual who is extolling or decrying the relative deadliness of any ammal, but one well-known hunter and naturalist answered the question in a manner that I find completely accurate. To paraphrase, "The rhino is no more dangerous than a drunken bus driver in a thick London fog."

Jim Sutherland, the great ivory hunter who was poisoned by natives, ranked the rhino last in the Big Five from his experiences in East Africa, saying that ". . . very little risk attaches to the hunting of the rhinoceros." He did, however, modify this somewhat by adding, "However, in any such classification, so much depends on the manner of hunting. . . ." Major Stigand, who, as mentioned, was terribly injured by a rhino in southeast Africa, still had the presence of reasonable conclusion to write the following: "A rhino is generally a very easily killed animal. If you can get him broadside on with a big bore he almost always sits down at once. Facing he is less easy to kill, and if moving, often a very difficult shot indeed." That seems pretty unbiased talk from a man who had a large portion of his chest ripped off by *uBejane*. In fact, I opine that it was Stigand who, through the unusually wide exposure he had to black rhino in very different terrain from the Sudan to Nyasaland, really caught the truth of the matter. Continuing, he wrote:

91

"In British East Africa, where he is plentiful and can be found in open country, there is nothing in killing a rhino. In Nyasaland and North Eastern Rhodesia, however, where he is more scarce and always found in thick grass or bush, he is really a very sporting animal to shoot. The natives there fear him more than any of the dangerous game, partly because he is really dangerous in their country, and partly because, owing to his scarcity, they have not grown accustomed to him." The Luangwa Valley is, incidentally, in the area of which Stigand speaks, Northern Rhodesia, now Zambia.

The rhino is kind of difficult to characterize in relation to the other Big Five. The others are mostly a peril to include on your guest list because they're smart, vengeful if given a chance, and better able to handle combat in the bush than the hunter is. The only equalizer is the rifle, and as has been observed, under most conditions it doesn't give all that big an edge. With the rhino, it's almost completely the opposite. He's dangerous and frequently deadly because he's so wonderfully dumb. He's so myopic that he can't tell a man from a tree at much more than seventy-five feet if the man is standing still. He's so territorial that the records of the Kenya Game Department show numerous cases of his charging young elephants and being tusked to death by their mothers in retaliation. Rhino were almost wiped out of one district in the 1930s because of this elephant–rhino war. Even with his armored skin, he is usually plagued with oozing sores simply from chafing against himself. There's even a Mashona legend I remember from the days in Rhodesia during the war, which claims that the rhino looks unkempt because he lost the fine needle that *Nkulunkulu*—God—gave him. The rhino was thus obliged to stitch up his skin sloppily with a thorn, which, combined with his bad eyesight, produced the animal equivalent of the straight man in a burlesque skit.

But there's nothing comical about *uBejane* when he's hot on your tail. If you're in range and he's in the mood, you'd better secure all the hatches, chum, because the weather's about to get rough. Don't bother asking why: Rhinos don't need a reason.

As a species, the rhino is no longer on the way out; the problem is that his haunts are disappearing. There'll still be plenty of *maBejane* safe from the poachers in the expanding parks, but as for my old hunting grounds, I suspect that it won't be all that long before the terror-thrill of wondering if something pushing two tons with a face full of horns won't pop out from behind the next bush will become a thing of the past, a problem of our grandfathers of which by then I will probably be one. When that day comes, I hope I'm hunting over the hill. When the bloody cattle take over and the turf is raped by the tender caress of John Deere and his friends; when the great *Ngamo* fig trees are sliced into plywood for packing crates; when the tribesmen are all Sanforized and watching feminine deodorant ads on color TV; I think I'd rather be with the rhino. But, for the moment, I reckon I'll just keep climbing.

4 ELEPHANT

MOTHS THE SIZE OF WOODCOCK mobbed the pressure lamp at the end of the dining hut table while a terminal moon suicided over the Luangwa River in an ecstasy of orange agony. Purple prose notwithstanding, it was one hell of a fine morning. Even Edgar Rice Burroughs would have overdosed on the absolute symphony of bush sounds; far, far across the dew-wet *tshani* grass on the other bank, a lion cursed his lady in phlegm-thickened grunts over the adenoidal honk of hippos in the big pool, accompanied through the blackness by soulful jackals and the full-mouthed insane asylum chitters, cackles, whoops, and screeches of a hunting pack of lucky hyenas. As the first diffusion of bloodshot sky leaked across the eastern horizon, a tom leopard provided the final touch with a series of seven ripsaw calls.

I was already awake when the alarm clock sounded off with the mechanical clatter of a soprano rattlesnake. For once, I had outsmarted the bloody thing, greeting the cool, smooth morning with pureness of brain if not soul. I had not entered into my clients' debate over the relative merits of Hennessey versus Oudemeester brandy and had thus been spared the shaggy teeth, the sunset eyes, and the little gnome who takes up skull trephining on so many safari mornings. Hail, happy dawn. Today we go elephant hunting.

Smug in the knowledge that I had shaved the night before, I already had on crisp, machete-creased bush shorts when the knock came to the *mopane* pole over the grass door of my *kaia.* *"Gena,"* I answered, and Martin came in with the cork-faced tea tray and perched it on the split slats of the table next to the bed. Stepping back smartly, he threw me an open-palmed British salute. Lord grant every man a Martin. Once a batman for a colonel of the crack Kenya outfit, the King's African Rifles, he could have taken over the Plaza's Palm Court with the same aplomb that he used to run my safari camps.

The sun came up straight out of *Lawrence of Arabia* as I stepped outside, my sockless desert boots throwing up tiny, mute explosions of red Zambian dust as I padded to the dining hut overlooking the river. Well into a raft of scrambles and campfire-broiled kudu fillet, I saw the two Texans wandering blearily through the early shadows. They managed their hot, black coffee well enough to wash down what seemed to be a handful of aspirins, topping the lot off with a cold Lion Lager each. As they revived, I reviewed the day's plans.

There had been three jumbos watering at a section of river some five miles away. By the spoor, one of them was a walloper if there is indeed any correlation between feet and tusks. What made me fairly sure that the *madalla,* or "old one," was a good tusker was that

98

the tracks of the two other males were those of younger *askari* bulls, or "soldiers," as they were called in the more northern but still traditional KiSwahili. Of course, this all-male arrangement held no direct bearing upon the ivory of the oldest beyond the fact that time is required to grow good tusks, but that was at least a starting point. Actually, few of the old rules held nowadays. Whereas big feet used to mean big tusks, now it frequently meant the opposite. The bulls with outsized feet had largely been tracked down and taken. Now it was the jumbos who had tracks small enough to discourage a fifty-mile hike who toted the heavy stuff, toe-dancing along with a face full of white telephone poles while most hunters sneered at the spoor. Still, maybe this one was a traditionalist.

The *askaris,* at least in African tradition, came along with the old boy when he'd had enough of the squalling of cows and *totos* to cut for greener pastures after his mating obligations, if he was up to it, forgive me the phrase. During their lengthy bushveld wanderings, the old chap would teach the younger *askaris* the things their mothers never told them about water holes, ripening *marula* fruit, and the thousand other things every young elephant should know. In return, the *askaris* would cover for the old boy, their ears sharp when his had gone muzzy, their trunks coiling like pythons in hot oil for the tendril of enemy smell, always ready to charge and destroy any threat to the Great Lord. Unfortunately, elephant hunters were high priority items. . . .

The *MaTexas,* as Silent rendered them in Fanagalo, seemed somewhat revived after a breakfast that would have done a survivor of the Donner Pass party proud. As they wandered off to collect their gear, I assembled my rifle, choosing the .470 Evans Nitro; twenty rounds of solids; belt knife; medical kit; and prayer book. The whole business fit perfectly in a small shoulder-carried container I had patterned after an ancient Scottish cartridge bag and had made up by Peter Becker down in Francistown at Botswana Game Industries. Among other doodads, the "possible" bag also contained M-80 thunderflashes, known to Americans as "ashcans"; a genuine Main Event David versus Goliath leather sling; a Swiss Army knife; water purification tablets; matches; cigarettes; enough prescription-obtained morphine Syrettes to numb a battalion (I had been hurt before without the benefit of artificial bliss); and eight sticks of steel-hard eland biltong, a sort of he-man version of jerky. There was also a flask of scotch, another of water, and enough tourniquets to hog-tie King Kong. As I am a pocket freak, there were a sufficient number of compartments, loops, and pouches in the bag's buffalo-hide interior that the whole works never rattled and at about six or seven pounds swung easily on Silent's shoulder. The super firecrackers, incidentally, were used to flush wounded lions or leopards. They were taped or tied to rocks or, in the case of the Luangwa Valley, which has no rocks, to a heavy cartridge, and were whirled off into the thick stuff with the sling. I suspect that they saved me a wonder of personal seamwork. Good for the complexion, I guess you might say.

There was time for a smoke with my hunting crew around the Land Rover before the clients came up. After double-checking the gear—air level in the spare tires; rope; axes; *skafu* box with sandwiches, cheese, crackers, teapot, and fixings; flax water sacks; and the rest of the drill—we watched the white coin of sun ratchet itself higher into the heavens. I would have preferred to have gotten out earlier, but the odds were that we wouldn't have a hope of catching up with the jumbos until they slowed up to rest at midday; in fact, I had told Martin to pack air mattresses and blankets in case we had to sleep on the spoor. As I field-stripped my smoke, the Americans made their usual bushy-tailed appearance.

I knew that it would be a good safari almost from the start. I had picked up the pair at the little airstrip at Mfuwe and driven four hours straight back to my camp at Nyampala, near the juncture of the Luangwa and Munyamadzi rivers. The next morning, after zero-ing the rifles, the taller client, Tex, placed a precise hole in a very fine kudu bull at two hundred yards with his .375. At fifty-five inches, the *mbalabala* was pretty close to the answer to a maiden's prayer, and we re-paired to camp after taking an impala for staff rations and a warthog for leopard bait. That night, Jack, the second client, who was better known as "Hoot" for his resemblance to the late Mr. Gibson, put a mess of kudu venison through the Bessemer Process and pro-duced a batch of white phosphorous *Tejano* chili that would have had a Hindu fire-eater screeching for suc-cor. Fortunately, I had been training on napalm-based curries for years and, opining that it *could* have been a bit more punchy, was instantly promoted to Honorary Texan.

Tex and Hoot (not their real names) were charac-ters straight out of Central Casting. Extremely suc-cessful businessmen, one was "in oil" and the other indirectly responsible for a couple of dozen million fast food burgers a year. That their overweight lug-gage ran better than four grand they accepted without a wince. The contents of their cases was questionable, at least in the mind of a mere Honorary Texan. Each had at least fifteen western-style hats featuring bands from ersatz Bird of Paradise to mating plumage *auerhahn*. Boots? One trunk looked like a sale at Kinney's. Never mind that they never wore them, the cowboy-style heels being impractical for stalking under Zambian conditions; there was everything from armadillo to ostrich to (I suspect) whooping crane and Tasmanian Devil. In their thirties, they were certainly no softies, and I'll promise you one thing, I'd hate to take on the Alamo if those boys were among the defenders. Lord, but they could shoot! Interestingly, their slightly flared sartorial splendor was not paralleled by their taste in guns: Mauser action .375s by Paul Jaeger and Griffin & Howe, plus a pair of custom .458s and a 12-gauge Beretta over/under for Tex and a Winchester Model 21 for Hoot. No fluff, just good lines and reliable top-quality ordnance. Speaking of ordnance, a good chunk of that four thousand dollars must have gone for the weight of twin cases of tequila, a remote Mexican brand that really blew the collective minds of my kitchen staff: Each bottle of the pale golden stuff sported a plump, whitish maguey worm in suspension. Palm grubs being among the favored delicacies of my black staff (they're not bad at all, I've tried them), Tex and Hoot were instantly and hugely appreciated when a bottle got low and the pickled larva was consumed by the Texans with much lip-smacking and showmanship. I am certain that there was never, at any time, any mental connection between my men and the fact that the clients were, at least technically, Americans.

Good clients take all the work out of professional hunting. There was never any bitching about whose shot it might be; hell, each fell all over the other like an Alphonse–Gaston act whenever sufficient applied sweat produced a trophy-quality, potential wall hanger. They played hard at night around the fire, but hungover or not, they were always at the *motogharri* when it was time to leave in the bleary dawn. They were always courteous to the hunting crew, almost to a fault, and brave as honey badgers, insisting that they be permitted to come along with me if things developed into the very rare nasty situation. The way they shot, that wasn't often.

Both Texans had picked up the traditional *Morni* greeting in Chenyanja and now boomed it with waves and grins to the blacks in the rear of the long-wheelbase 'Rover. Of course, they pronounced it "morning," but it didn't seem worth the trouble to have a short Berlitz course. Silent, my old ferret-eyed gunbearer, took Hoot's mesquite-stocked Winchester and handed it to Quiza while Invisible, Silent's heavyset brother, slapped a hand as calloused as a rhino's foot around Tex's .458 and pocketed a box of solids. Sekala, my field skinner, smoked a thumb-thick tube of black shag tobacco wrapped in the political section of a Mozambique newspaper, passing it back to Javuli, his assistant. After all had muttered their polite *morni* and *eeehhh* to the *MaTexas*, I slipped the clutch and we headed upriver to see if the bulls had watered the previous night.

They had.

The spoor was about a quarter mile past the trail they had left yesterday, but there was no doubt that these were the same three bulls. Since the far side of the Luangwa was a protected area outside the hunting concession, it's just possible that the tuskers had become a touch complacent by watering in a routine manner; possibly they thought they were on some sort of Game Department welfare with potential local vil-

103

lage banana plots thrown in as food stamps. The spoor we discovered after covering the mile and a half from the spot where we had left the Land Rover couldn't have been over three hours old.

After an hour of tracking alternately through the sere September-gray grass and huge stands of mixed yellow acacia, brachystegia, and *mopane* woodlands, a slick, sun-glistening pile of whatever you wish to tactfully call the stuff that comes out of the backside of an elephant proved still quite near body heat when Silent, Invisible, and I poked tentative forefingers into it. Considerably bigger than a breadbox, the stack of droppings was, as Silent also pointed out, from the Old Boy. Badly chewed strips of the bark that lines the pristine slivers of tender branch shoots had been swallowed and had passed along their merry route almost unscathed because the once rough grinding 9-pound molars of the bull were now worn as smooth as the bottom of an enamel bathtub. It was probably the bull's last set of perhaps six; when they could no longer crush his rough fodder fit for digestion, it wouldn't be long before emaciation set in, and then even less time before the Big Peanut Pile in the Sky. Elephants don't simply die of old age, they starve to death when their teeth give out. Not all that many generations ago, we probably did the same thing. Even the concept of burying human dead is perhaps no more than fifty-thousand to seventy-five thousand years old, and not many hungry tribesmen spent a lot of time making gruel for the nonproducers. Sorry for the culture shock, but remember that Wall Street and Madison Avenue still work the same way. . . .

It was Quiza, toting Hoot's .458 by the barrel over his shoulder, who froze first. His head, cocked like a pointer who has spotted a snootful of quail, was rigid under the tattered World War I aviator's helmet; his hand was raised for silence. Long the victim of partial nerve deafness from muzzle blasts, I couldn't hear what had first caught his ear. As we all stood rather ridiculously balanced on one foot or in whatever posture his hiss had caught us, we strained over the interwoven mat of bushveld sounds to filter out whatever Quiza had heard. Slowly, his arm swung across his body as he stared at the ground in concentration, his right arm pointing off to our right front like the tip of a divining rod calibrated for elephants.

Seconds tiptoed over the chirp of crickets and grasshoppers and the racket of a nearby colony of weaver birds. Almost out of sight overhead, a bataleur eagle keened a blade-edged cry that quivered on the hot morning air. A tiny splintering of grass stems crunched as Tex lost his half-balance and almost sprawled forward on his face. His observations in muttered Spanish were highly colorful. A full minute went by, then another. I was just about to wave the hunters on when Silent snapped his fingers softly and pointed. I still couldn't hear it, but he made the motion of breaking a stick and indicated a shady 10-acre tract of hardwoods a half-mile away. Then there was no doubt. A short, sharp blast of trumpet sounded clearly, not a sound of alarm or fear, but just the sort of toot relaxed jumbos give one another when they're in high spirits. They might as well have fired a flare.

Lighting a cigarette, I saw the smoke waft in the direction of the puff of spores that Invisible tapped from a round fungus: Almost into our faces—it seemed perfect.

Motioning my men into a huddle, I had the clients check the loads of their rifles and detached the leather sling of my .470 so that it wouldn't get hung up in bush. I broke the action and checked the big Kynoch solids, slipping them back into the chambers with the peculiar metallic hollow drainpipe "tonk" that only loading a double rifle makes. Invisible, Quiza, and Javuli hunkered down and lit their extra edition cigarettes, knowing from experience that I would leave them here in the open to avoid unnecessary danger. Three may be a crowd elsewhere, but four is a positive mob when stalking jumbo in heavy cover. Silent would lead off until we were within good range, then drop from the head to the rear while I set up the shot. The worn twenty-dollar American gold double eagle that Hoot carried as a lucky piece hadn't been working very hard that morning; he lost the toss. Tex would take the shot, if we got one and the bull turned out to be toothy.

From the first fringe of the stand of hardwoods, things didn't look especially peachy. Most of the grove was mature *mopane,* which although leafy was still green, blotting out visibility above while dormant. Dead grass lower down closed off our view like the sides of a duck blind. Every few steps, we paused to listen, the feeding sounds of the three bulls more than a little intimidating as they tore off thick branches for their tender leaves with the casual ease of a kid pulling the wings off a fly. From about eighty yards ahead, a low rumble sounding like a very distant mutter of thunder could be discerned intermittently. Once thought to be the noise of moonshine-vat stomachs doing what came naturally with hundreds of pounds of fodder, this weird sound is now accepted by most hunters and scientists to be a proximity signal, a way of locating each other in very thick bush while (possibly) the elephants' hearing is a bit dampened by the sound of their own chewing. That it can apparently be stopped instantly when suspicion of danger pops up seems to bear this out. Ever try to squelch a stomach rumble in the middle?

From the stacks of steaming condominium-sized pasture patties, it appeared that the three bulls had been feeding and frolicking here for some hours. Quietly reaching down, Silent and I each felt the still-wet white skeletons of bark-stripped branches, the slime of saliva and sap slick and slippery still. Of course, it was just habit; the elephants were no more than fifty yards ahead in the vegetable gloom, their massive creaking and swishing sounds holding our completely undivided attention. Too close to risk a whisper, I signed to the Texans to keep quiet, which was probably unnecessary as they were both slightly bug-eyed and practically lathered with honest, nervous sweat. The closest either had come to a wild elephant was a billiard table or some friend's trophy room. If they weren't scared they were either stupid, uninformed, or decided suicides. I knew them to be none of the above.

I made a fist and pushed my thumb along the top of it. Tex caught on and eased off the safety of his rifle, carefully carrying it in the automatically protected position of a man long used to handling firearms, muzzle up and across his chest. Silent disappeared to the rear, the flash of his spear blade swallowed by the murk that as easily concealed his dusty, dark hide. With the exaggerated steps of stealthy mimes, we advanced, edging aside any of the deadwood of trees held in suspension by the deathbed of dry grass. At thirty yards, there was still not the slightest suggestion of a trio of the world's largest land mammals, only the continuing crunch of lunch leaking through the bush like audio-osmosis.

It is impossible to try to convey to someone who has seen his elephants in zoos or even in the open spaces of game parks and reserves that the very immensity of the bloody things acts as perfect camouflage. A biggish bull will average about eleven feet at the top of the shoulder and some twenty feet in length, depending on how the measurement is calculated, and will certainly represent well over one hundred square feet of hide in profile. Even the most famous professional ivory hunters have, in reasonably open country, executed termite hills with perfect brain and heart shots, mistaking them for jumbos. As most game is recognized by outline or portions thereof, it may be understood that the sheer size of an elephant's silhouette, when broken by even what later will seem surprisingly thin bush, renders him almost literally a 6-ton will-o'-the-wisp. The effective result of this phenomenon is that most jumbo are shot close not only because it's far more sporting than potting one at long range but also because there's no choice. More's the point, if you're close enough to him, he's also more than close enough to you to rank in destructive potential with a hair-trigger cobalt bomb. The meek may well inherit the earth, but they won't spend much time elephant hunting if they do.

The shade-cooled wind held true as we inched up, my heart giving the odd little flutter-thump it always does when the waft of fresh stable smell and hot urine reaches up into my sinuses and gives a tweak. I glanced at Tex, just behind and off my elbow and then back at Hoot, who had a salami length of tongue caressing the far reaches of his outsized roan mustache in complete concentration. Good ones, the pair. Foot by foot, we sneaked forward, stopping every step to stare at the miasma of *miombo* that caused our eyes to water with strain. The bulls sounded close enough to slap with a canoe paddle; even the airy wheeze of breath through their trunks sounded as if it were in our hip pockets. We were getting close. Too close. At this distance, there would only be fractions of dietetic seconds to make a decision to run or shoot, climb or pray, or just drop stone dead from accumulated apprehension if the wind shifted. As it turned out, the wind didn't have to shift.

We were within twenty yards before I spotted the first hint of motion: A gray hawser as thick as a bridge support snaked upward and goosed along the green fluff of a plume of leaves, finally wrapping around it and tearing it free with a rustle. As I stared over the half-raised Evans, the line of a foreleg came fuzzily into focus, shifting slightly as the bushel of *mopane* disappeared somewhere into the loading end of the jumbo. The low rumble sounded again and was answered from a few yards to my right. As slowly as possible, I fished out the small binoculars and screwed the focus adjustment all the way down. If using field glasses at twenty paces seems optical overkill, you've never hunted elephants. With the vein of each leaf standing out as if varicose, I was able to jigsaw out the top of the bull's head and an impression of darkly earth-and-sapstained ivory. But it wasn't enough. There was still no way to tell if it was the old bull or not; just too much stuff was in the way.

Without taking down the glasses, I reached across, took a pinch of Tex's Abercrombie bush jacket and gently tugged him to my side. He looked as if somebody were holding a straight razor up his nose. Unlike another client under similar circumstances who simply forgot where he was and uttered a full-mouthed "Holy Jesus!" that would have made a reborn preacher blush with the obvious sincerity of the awed remark, Tex kept mum. (To my continued astonishment, the earlier client's fervent invocation of at least one-third of the Trinity didn't get anybody killed. The two elephants in question must have been as astounded as I. They left, posthaste, for the Carpathian Alps, where they are possibly still in residence. Too bad; one was an orthodontist's dream.)

With the wind holding true, we stayed in that spot for fully six or seven minutes, trying to figure out who was who among the bulls. I finally got a decent look at the chap on the right and saw that he carried only about thirty pounds a side of bicuspids; not worth the trouble. That left the one dead ahead and, by the sounds, another farther beyond him, the whole group forming a rough L with the two nearest at the base of the letter and at the tip of the bottom stroke. At last, after what seemed a double decade, the nearest must have decided that he would move on for dessert and swung away, showing a very good loop of tusk as he turned. It had to be the Old Boy, but now he was facing almost dead away and offering no kind of shot at all. Of course, had I been hunting for the game department or controlling crop raiders, I would have hipped or spined him, but then there is nothing at all in common between systematic ecologically based reduction hunting or culling and sport hunting. Nobody wants to take a pose and answer the question of where he shot his elephant by allowing that he had pasted it in the arse! This shot is known as the "Texas neck shot" or the "reverse brain shot." Not done in nicer circles, I'm pleased to advise. . . .

I was just trying to figure out what our next move might be when the zoological equivalent of the explosion of the Tunguska Meteor occurred a few yards away. A short startled yelp of human fear barked from what must have been the far side of the wood, instantly joined by the bellows, screams, and blares of the brass section of the elephant contingent. What the hell! No time to figure it out now, with a brownish-gray mountain the size of a townhouse rolling straight down on us as if on an unshackled trailer from the right while another began to darken the daylight gaps between the grass and leaves from dead ahead. I shouted something I doubt I learned in Sunday School and waved my arm, snicking off the Evans' safety almost unconsciously. Tex and Hoot howled some very interesting things usually categorized as expletives, although that definition might have been a touch mild for the circumstances. The right-hand bull heard us and sheared off after coming to a complete halt at about nine yards. I had him lined up for five hundred grains of prefrontal surprise just as starters, and he seemed to know it, angling sharply to the side to disappear into the wood.

We were luckier with the big bull. He broke at about fifteen yards, immediately to our front, heading ever so slightly across our bow. He was super. He was huge. He had teeth like Mae West had . . . well, he was a beauty. "Chest him, for Christ's sake, Tex," I shouted over the confusion and saw the Texan's rifle line up. As the tusker rushed by close enough to consider fixing bayonets, Tex fired.

We were too near to hear the bullet strike, and I saw no sign of impact. I heard the slither of steel on steel as he worked the bolt, the bright tube of spent brass flipping away. Swinging at the decreasing angle of the huge shoulder, I saw the muzzle flash of the .458 erupt again just as the bull passed behind a thick pig-iron–tough *mopane* tree, a pie plate of bark and splintered white wood pulverizing under the slug's impact. And then, the bull was gone.

I covered the front in case the third bull, the remaining *askari,* came for us until I finally heard him crashing away out through the side of the trees. All gone. No more. Finished. *Kuisha. Quedile.* Tex, a man who could practically drive nails at three hundred yards offhand, who regularly tripled on quail with his .410 pump gun, had missed his tusker broadside at a paced-off eleven yards.

Nobody said much as we plunked down where we were and lit three smokes out of my flat-pack of Matinees. Tension hung around us like a skunk scent of frustration, clinging like a cloud of static electricity. And then, a low rumble started right next to me, making me snatch for my rifle. When I saw it was Tex, laughing with tears cutting clear rivulets through the sweat and dirt of his cheeks, it became infectious. In a few seconds, Hoot and I joined him, collapsing in uncontrollable whoops, rocking with smothered howls and snatches at breath.

It was more than just the relief of nervous tension. The tall American seeming really to be tickled. Finally, in a strangled voice, he managed to gasp, "Whooo! I *missed* him! I actually *missed* him!" A new spasm shook him and we all dissolved in a fresh attack of mirth.

"What happened?" Hoot asked as tactfully as possible.

"Hit the trigger by mistake before I could get down on him," replied Tex with a watermelon-slice grin. "Imagine *that*! I actually missed him! And then, just as I squeezed off when I had things under control, the goddam tree stepped into the way!"

A few minutes later, we discovered that the three

bulls had been spooked by getting wind of two local tribesmen who happened to enter the wood upwind of us, unaware of the elephants, to look for wild honey. They said they were sorry, I don't doubt it. They would have had more red meat than they could have carried, but I couldn't really be very angry. It was, after all, a simple mistake. They didn't know that either our party or the jumbos were in the trees. Silent, Invisible, and Quiza had had a good view of the best tusker as he came out of the cover and literally high-tailed it for the far horizon. My guess, based on the long glimpse I had had, and corroborated by their gape-jawed stares, put him at about eighty pounds a side. Considering that anything over fifty pounds per tusk is considered decent, the one that got away was a genuine monster. That Tex had the sportsmanship to consider the happenings hilarious, particularly when the joke was really on him at an averaged-out eight hundred dollars a day, seemed to me a great example of the sense of fair play that good hunters so often display. Of course, others would have been heartbroken or even accusatory that I hadn't decked the bull. I couldn't by law or by inclination. The only time I ever fired my rifle was to protect life or to anchor a *wounded* animal that, in my opinion, might escape to become a menace or die alone in agony. In any case, both Tex and Hoot eventually did collect their elephants, Hoot's tipping in at a nicely paired fifty-five and fifty-eight pounds and Tex's a bigger but more lopsided sixty-four and fifty-one.

Two weeks later, near the end of the safari, Hoot and Tex were revelling around the campfire with their usual outrageous jokes and stories when the conversation tilted back to that day in the stand of trees. Hoot, never one to pass up a friendly broadsword between

Tex's ribs, brought up the incident of the missed jumbo. Tex lit a fresh imported Winston and stared briefly into the fire. Taking a toss of his tequila, he let a small grin play over his angular face.

"Hell, man," drawled Tex, "that's what conservation's all about."

Hunting elephant on foot in thick cover has long been called "The Classic of Big Game Hunting," and you'd have to lather up a pretty fair argumentative sweat to convince me that it isn't the absolute truth. Unless you've walked the dry, heat-rash, asbestos-tongued miles, crawled the worlds of wait-a-bit thorn, felt your heart pushing up into your throat until you thought it would be pounded into chicken liver paté by the pulse stamping in your ears like a 400-pound Flamenco dancer, you will never really appreciate the unique mixture of apprehension, exhilaration, and pure terror that the sport can produce. All of the Big Five are dangerous; there are more than enough weathering headstones to frank that. Still, there's something about the sheer size and irresistibility of an angry bull elephant that places the pursuit of ivory in a category of its own.

To be logical, it's probably the impossible bulk coupled with a method of hunting that requires such close approach that scares bright people so thoroughly. Heavy rifles have a way of feeling like BB guns when you walk up to a 12,000- or 14,000-pound chunk of trouble on his home ground and gape up at a grayish-red eye ten or more feet off the ground. More than a few adult diapers have been dampened by the most modest expression of vocal elephantine displeasure and, when things turn from fuzzy to furry to downright hairy, it suddenly becomes horribly clear why even some of the best-known professional ivory hunters have lost their nerves and frozen during a close-quarter charge. Some had their heads torn off and pitched like unraveling baseballs fifty or more yards away; others were held down with a forefoot that crushed their chests with the same magnified crunch of a crisp, gleaming beetle under a riding boot. Quite a few got to play along somewhat longer as old jumbo picked off their arms and legs and flipped them in bloody arcs through the bush. Some were beaten to death—what an understatement!—against trees, rocks, termite heaps, and other convenient items until they were sliding skin bags full of bloody, bone-splintered mush. A few, who were the intended victims of a wide variety of tusking techniques, even lived. The great Neumann was gored through the chest and arm while an elephant's forehead rasped the skin off his face for fifteen minutes of premature eternity. Carl Akeley, who birthed the American Museum of Natural History's African Hall, got caught by a jumbo and was so rearranged that he was left in the icy high-altitude rain of Kenya's Aberdares Mountains for five hours by his corpse-shy native entourage. Jim Sutherland, one of the most fabled of the followers of the "Ivory Trail," was once trunk-thrown and landed on the bull's back! Hanging on for literal dear life, he managed to grab an overhead branch and then dropped to the ground and followed up the elephant when he found his rifle. "I killed that swine," he wrote to a pal later, but he couldn't sit down or sleep on his back for a couple of weeks.

Training for elephant hunting is fairly uncomplicated. Whereas sheep and mountain goat hunters concentrate on such interesting pretrip pursuits as hanging by their teeth, push-ups, running the stairs of their office buildings, and eating wheat germ, honey, and yogurt, getting fit for a confrontation with a jumbo requires essentially one skill: walking. Elephants ease along at about the speed of an Olympic sprinter, and that's when they're not going anywhere in particular. Bell, who bears no reintroduction here, wore out a pair of custom hunting-walking boots every two weeks, and that was in the days when there were stacks of trusting jumbo in practically untouched country. Sutherland, who may have been a little more practical, had relays of runners to carry him in a portable hammock called a *machila* whenever possible. Whatever the locomotion principle, even in the early part of this century ivory meant big bucks, provided you lived to spend them.

Still, elephants require footwork in the most elemental sense of the word. Packing the equivalent of internal fire hydrants, they don't have to water more than every few days, but it is essentially the necessity of ingesting an incredible bulk of low-energy-yield vegetable foods that keeps them hoofing for such great distances. Elephants don't do a hell of a lot besides eat and chase idiots, which takes up most of their waking hours. Some authorities have claimed that they never lie down to sleep, but I disagree, having twice seen both cows and bulls snoring fit to peel the plaster, zonked out on their sides. A fellow pro I once did a safari with won a sort of dubious immortality among the brethren by presuming that a snoozing *Njovu,* as they are called in Zambia, was dead. He actually got up to a standing position on the bum of the dozing bull before he realized the impropriety of his ways. Luckily, the jumbo apparently thought him a bad dream and spared him the first instructions of the recipe for

116

creamed *bwana*. Incidentally, the pro in question was killed two years later because of a much lesser transgression against another elephant. I wasn't there, but I was told that what was left could have been shipped back to Europe in not much more than one padded mailer. One must perforce admire the thoroughness of the irritated *Loxodonta*.

As a standard-design organism featuring a leg in each corner, the elephant is an interesting mixture of strengths and weaknesses from the viewpoint of the hunter. That savannah elephants may have ears measuring seven feet from base to top is a decent indication that the organ wasn't put there for trimming. The hearing of a jumbo, especially if he is in a suspicious mood—which occupies large segments of his time in most places—is probably on a fair par with the electronic hearing of the Distant Early Warning System. Jumbos foul up when they fail to interpret correctly the cause of some bush sounds, which from time to time prove painfully to have been created by Chicago businessmen and crusty but not-so-benign *bwanas*. Beyond the obvious sound-impulse gathering properties of slightly less than sixty square feet of ears—poetically shaped in a spooky reproduction of the continent of Africa—the big flappers are a most effective way to cool the blood, working on the radiator principle. With a network of veins thicker than a close-up of my hungover right eye, the mature Dumbo's wings probably cool a couple of quarts of blood with a casual flap.

Some have said that elephants see pretty well, but I have no evidence of their having an effective range beyond a dozen yards. Motion, of course, is noticed at considerably greater distances and is to be avoided. With a correct wind, most tuskers can be approached startlingly close, *provided* (and that's a very big conditional word) they haven't smelled, heard, or otherwise sensed the presence of humans. Birds such as oxpeckers and egrets can often be frustratingly alert sentries, putting a tusker into flight long before a shot can be set up.

Wind is the most important element in the stalking of elephant, as far and away the most effective organ is the trunk. Ivory hunters have written of elephants crossing a path where their bearers had walked the day *before* and becoming agitated to the extent of picking up the tainted earth and running off in alarm. One told the undoubtedly true tale of a small calf picking up the hunter's ground spoor, snatching up a bit of dirt, and toddling over to Mumsie for an explanation of the weird odor. Fortunately, at least for the hunter who was more or less surrounded by a herd of cows and calves in still air, the Old Lady must have had her mind on duplicate bridge or tatting. Another hunter, in what was then Northern Rhodesia's Luangwa Valley, where I did a few mating dances, had a *toto* actually sniff him down and touch his face, only to run off to his mother in panic. In a word, if you don't have the wind, you won't have elephants.

To turn a ragged phrase, it's what makes elephant hunting elephant hunting that makes it so dangerous. When the close approaches required are compounded by the great intelligence and unbelievably destructive powers of the critters, it becomes clear why so many elephant hunters got themselves spectacularly killed or immediately switched careers to less spooky pursuits such as snake charming or bomb disposal. The key word is "territory." When you're sweating and half-peeing all over the personal space of a bull elephant, you are clearly an intruder. Elephants don't like intruders, and when they find them close enough to tell the brand of last night's salad dressing, they have a decided tendency to charge as a defense mechanism. I can only liken the feeling to the one I get as an Anglo-Irish American when a member of a differently oriented culture insists on shoving his face into mine for the simplest conversation, thumbing and tugging my lapel for emphasis until I have an overwhelming urge to either run or push him off to a safe psychological distance, where I will again feel that my territory is not jeopardized. I really hate any invasion of my "personal" area, the perhaps two feet that surrounds me in some sort of psychic cocoon.

Under hunting conditions the practical result of this territorial urge is that jumbos are far more prone to charge unwounded than any other member of the Big Five under like circumstances. The trick, which comes only with experience, is to be able to tell which is a bluff charge and which isn't. This is like playing Twenty Questions for your life, because elephants aren't all that reliable. Or perhaps dominoes would be a better parallel, because if you don't work things out correctly, you go directly to the boneyard. To simplify, if a tusker happens to look over his shoulder and notice a couple of khaki-clad figures at about ten yards, he'll probably realize that safety more likely lies in a flat-out, no-kidding annihilation of the intruders than a break for more distant cover. In a game reserve, where he may be a bit more used to such breaches of etiquette, a great demonstration of how big he is and how small you are may do the trick. Don't bet on it. Ex-game warden Johnny Uys did and he is now among the deeply lamented.

The various fatal shots on elephants are among the most debated and least understood of the deadly points on any dangerous game. Probably with good reason, too, for elephants are not shaped quite like anything else. Perhaps the old bit about the secret of sculpting is apropos: Get a helluva big piece of marble and chip away anything that doesn't look like an elephant.

Probably the brain shot is considered the great classic, especially from the frontal angle. Properly placed with the use of sufficient gun and nondisrupting solids, it is spectacularly effective if it burrows through the brain, an oblong item about the size of an underinflated rugby ball or a loaf of rye bread. The big misunderstanding is just where the brain is to be found.

A rather strange illustration of the (presumably) frontal brain shot appears in the frontispiece of the revered Lonsdale Library's *Big Game Shooting in Africa* (ed. Major H. C. Maydon), which contains a slather of chapters done by practically anybody who had spent extensive time hunting in Africa before the 1932 publication date. The generic chapter on elephant hunting was contributed by Denis D. Lyell, a very reliable author-soldier-hunter whose views and pen-marked illustrations of the side-angle shots on elephant I completely agree with. The strange picture in question shows a toothpick-tusked bull across a bit of water at a range of perhaps thirty yards. The trunk is raised, the ears flared, and the head well up. To be sure, the upper heart shot is within deadly reach, but there is another penned circle right at the base of the jumbo's lifted trunk, just at the top of the mouth and right between the tusks where they emerge from their sockets. Perhaps it's supposed to be a frontal jaw shot or something else weird, but it's clearly not going to come within a couple of feet of the brain! I grant that a big bullet practically down the throat wouldn't perk up the toughest bull, but this is about the strangest shot I ever saw described. Personally, I'd stick a good solid through the trunk and on into the brain or, preferably, wait for him to shift position, lower his trunk, or otherwise clear a way for the bullet's passage. However, you *can* shoot through the trunk; I've done it several times under duress.

The elusiveness of the frontal brain shot is well illustrated by the fact that the celebrated Sir Samuel Baker *never* decked an African elephant with a frontal brain shot, although he killed plenty with body shots. Actually, at the time he took up African exploration and hunting, he had killed more Asian elephants—mostly in Ceylon—than any man in history. I've never shot an Indian elephant (*Elephas maximus*) but the conformation of the skull seems to indicate that the brain is not situated in quite the same position as that of the African elephants. This might have stickied Baker's wicket a touch.

Learning the frontal shot has some interesting ramifications for a person who makes a living as a hunter or, as was also my case, an elephant cropping officer. As with most matters pertaining to dangerous game, there is no room for the trial and error method. If you try and err, you usually don't get a chance to try again, at least not in this world.

Bob Langeveld, who has now taken over three thousand elephants in his cropping duties for Zambia, Zaire, Tanzania, and KwaZulu, was my mentor in learning the frontal shot and that he is a master of it is beyond question. Hell, he's killed more than three times as many elephants as did Karamojo Bell and most of the other great ivory and control hunters of decades ago. I've spoken of his formula before, but it is worth repeating here. Bob envisions a straight line or stick that passes through the earholes. The exterior aiming point for the brain from the front angle varies widely because elephants don't hold their heads still. Also, as the distance from elephant to hunter increases or decreases, a different vertical angle is created; the closer, the more acute. Bob pays no attention to the outside of the animal, only seeing that imaginary pole passing through the head and shooting for the middle of it. I've never seen him miss a frontal shot and to the contrary have seen him cool five chargers in a row with his .470 (he now uses a .500/.465), stacking them line astern with the head of one nearly touching the tail of the one ahead. Impressive gunnery!

The side brain shot is really a piece of cake if you can keep your guts out of your pants and your heart below your ears. The ideal angle is from ever so slightly behind the animal, no more than a few degrees aft of his head. From this position the earhole, where the bullet from behind should go, is clearly visible as an orifice. If you are directly to the side or slightly ahead, it's marked by a dark crease in the skin fold. The shot should fall somewhere along the line between eye and ear, closer to the ear from rearward and closer to the eye from a more frontal plane. Also, like the frontal, the vertical angle must be remembered and the point of aim lowered a few inches if the jumbo is towering over you at very close range or brought up smack on the ear-eye line at a bit more yardage.

In considering either the frontal or side brain shots, try to think of a box with a smallish sphere suspended in the center on a stiff wire that keeps it in place no matter which way the box is tilted. You couldn't care less which part of the surrounding box you hit, for the ball in the center is the target. So ignore the outside of the box and the outside of the elephant, visualizing only the interior target. This is such an effective method that I must say that I cannot recall ever having had a frontal brain shot not kill instantly, and I've certainly taken several hundred elephants with it. God forbid that this be taken as chest thumping; I only use the frontal if I'm three times overpositive that I can place it exactly. That means getting in close enough to smell the peanuts on his breath rather than any needle-threading marksmanship on my part. On the other hand, I think the side brain shot is easier, but, despite practice, I have muffed this shot several times. Fortunately, the side brain shot is not normally consistent with the circumstances of a charge, whereas the frontal nearly always is.

A heap has been written about the shock effect of bullets that strike near the brain but miss it. John "Pondoro" Taylor's "knock out" formula of bullet impact was calculated on how long a nearly brained jumbo would be out cold under these circumstances. I really can't figure how a man with the experience of Taylor, who was certainly no cringing violet when it came to taking on dangerous game, drew such positive conclusions given the tremendous range of reactions that the same shot on different elephants can produce. For a certainty, an elephant may be knocked cold by the concussion of a slug skirting the brain, but under what seem to be identical conditions, the next one won't do more than toss his head and come for you. I have been in on the killing of two tailless bulls with the healed wounds neat as surgery from somebody's hunting knife, the taking of the tail being the traditional proof of ownership of the carcass. One of the pros I worked with in Zambia had the interesting experience of actually being seated on a bull who woke up from a closely missed brain shot. Fortunately for my pal, the jumbo merely stood up and ran, the hunter falling off to the side. He still has the tail.

Cropping is a great testing ground for theory. I recall once, in 1969, going on a cropping expedition with Bob Langeveld and Robin Jones, then—and perhaps still, for all I know—resident game ranger for the area around the Mfuwe Lodge on the Luangwa. Robin was a delightful gentleman, yet at that time without much experience with jumbo, and Bob had agreed to let him get his hand in when next we went out cropping. Robin borrowed ten or so rounds of my .375 solids, being low on his ration, and came along with Bob, Bob's assistant, Ricetime, and me one afternoon when we had only a dozen or so to cull. I can't be certain if Robin was a good shot or not, as I'd never seen him shoot until that day, but he certainly wasn't short on guts. Following Bob's example of running straight up to the biggest cow, which led the herd, Robin hoofed himself almost up the thing's bum, shouting at it for some fifty yards to charge. This old cow wasn't having any of it until Robin got almost close enough to touch her. It was a cool performance from a man who had seen what jumbo can do when displeased. The old *Njovu* swung around, madder than a snake, and thundered straight at the ranger. He raised the rifle and smacked her plop in the chops with a 300-grain persuader. I promise you, although the slug hit right where her trunk joined her forehead, she never blinked. At about six yards, he swatted her again, just a bit higher, but still not far enough up to get the brain. She was literally throwing her shadow over Robin when Bob fired from behind him with a .470 and Ricetime touched off from the side at the same microsecond with his .404 issue Jeffery's. The cow dissolved under the twin brain shots, but had Robin not been backed up, he might have received an airmail ride home.

You may say that this is proof that the .375 is inadequate, but I've seen the same thing happen with .458s, .460s, .476s, .470s, and once with a .577 Nitro, so I think the blame again lies with the shock theory rather than the cartridges. Would the .600 Nitro with 900-grain bullets have done better? Taylor reckoned it would keep an elephant unconscious up to half an hour! Maybe, but for sure not always.

Body shots on jumbo are by no means to be scorned as something less than classic, being reliably deadly: they cover a fatal area at close range that provides a decent certainty of preventing nonfatally wounded animals. I spent a recent evening poring through some diaries and journals, rain-smeared and sun-bleached ring binders that I always wrote up in camp before the dinner cry of *"Chakula!"* or *"Skafu!"* depending upon where I was. I have, in fact, never had any experience with a wounded elephant that had to be followed up. I'm sure the contingent that is less than charmed with the pastime would reach the immediate conclusion that I shoot my clients' game for them.

No way.

I'm a walking, two-legged, balding, heartburned, hypertensive insurance policy who doubles as head-waiter, guide, bridge partner, confidant, marriage counselor, sanitary expert, local ornithologist, botanist ("yeah, it causes a rash"), gunsmith, drinking buddy, linguist, and bodyguard, among other duties. I am also obliged by law to try to kill any wounded game, including elephants, that might otherwise, after a shot that is not fatal, turn murderous upon escape. That's my job. If it's hit but not killed, no matter what the species, it counts against very expensive licenses and even more valuable hunting time. Moreover, the animal may turn the non-penny-awful equivalent of rogue. If it either comes for us or runs from us after being hit, I'm supposed to put it down. That's what I *do*. And if you know anything about the lifestyle of professional hunters, you will quickly agree that it is impossible that we do it for the money. . . . I dearly hope nobody interprets the foregoing as any form of presumed apology.

I can recall several instances in which the chest shot to the elephant's general shoulder area, even with the .375, proved astoundingly effective. Once was in Zambia, when I had taken over a *torero,* a well-known bullfighter, from another professional for reasons that I do not care to relive. A runner came into camp courtesy of Paul Nielssen, of whom I have spoken elsewhere as having been badly mauled by a lion, advising that a pair of good tuskers had been spotted some miles from his camp on the Luangwa. Paul had seen them personally and, as his client had a full bag of jumbo, saw no reason to waste them. The spoor was a day old when we picked it up past dawn the next morning.

It was October, hot as passion and dry as Nevada. We marched for bloody ever before the first dung became remotely fresh, with my cursing Paul for his kindness the whole way. We were so far out of the Luangwa Valley that the Muchingas foothills, piles of loose stone and dirt the size of mine tailings, dragged us back, and dust mixed with the ooze of our sweat to form a devil's necktie that rasped away our throats and necks until they were raw. Still, the indistinct spoor of the two bulls was enough to keep us going, big, promising feet that, confirming Paul's sighting, meant two shootable—nay, trophy—bulls.

Silent had the spoor, stalking along on spindle shanks like a preoccupied praying mantis, never speaking but occasionally pointing to a small rock here and there that had been tipped by a massive foot, showing a damper, less-weathered side. We went straight up the side of one of these steep hillocks following spoor about four hours old, moving fairly casually because of the age of the tracks. Not fifty feet from the top, Silent froze, slowly raising his hand. I looked and saw the arse end of a jumbo, facing aft about 120 degrees away. I guess it *was* hot, as the two elephants had quit trekking and were resting during the heat of midday in the thin mixture of bush and scraggly trees that were making a poor living from the starvation soil between the rocks. I collared the bullfighter and put him into position, trying to spot the second jumbo. Only one could be seen from where we perched, but he turned his head and showed us that he was very worthwhile, about sixty pounds a side. To his credit, the *matador de toros* executed a superb angle brain shot from below with his Brno .458 Czech rifle, which collapsed the tusker like a popped paper bag. Perhaps *too* good a shot, as the bull floundered and came over the edge of the loose rock straight down at us, creating a trail-size avalanche of stones and boulders as he fell. I don't know about anybody else present, but it scared the hell out of me!

Fortunately, his body was caught up on a finger of stone and not deposited in our midst. Looking up again, I noticed more movement as a second bull flashed across a 20-yard opening in the cover. *"Mátale,"* I yelled in Spanish, another of my failings, and the bullfighter stuck the jumbo a teensy bit aft with another .458. The glimpse I had had of the animal clearly showed him to be even better than the first, and my client had two elephant licenses, the second available at substantial cost. The old, familiar whuff of dried wallow mud went up like a tracer round and I knew the bull to be *probably* lung-hit. But I wasn't sure. Running at whatever top speed I had left, I cleared the crest and zigzagged between thick stuff until I saw the bull heading through some light bush about two hundred yards away with his accelerator wide open. That he wasn't blowing blood made me decide instantly to stick him, as that much exercise would have shown pink trunk-foam signs of his being lung-shot. I can close my eyes as I write this and see him now over the shallow vee of the iron sights.

He was running—elephants don't really run but they sure walk like hell—to my left, quite visible as I locked in on him. I held to the exact fore-edge of his chest in the middle of his body, trying specifically for neither heart nor lung but hoping to break a shoulder and anchor him. I squeezed off and because of the recoil never saw where the round hit. Wherever, it was for sure the right spot, as the elephant bull dropped as if dynamited! Whether the solid was deflected by a shoulder bone and severed the spine or merely grenaded bone shards through his vitals—or maybe the same instant it hit him he dropped dead from the bullfighter's shot—I'll never know. He fell, as is the rule, on the same side I shot him. But, brother, he sure died in one impressive hurry. If I hadn't known better, I'd have sworn he'd been brained.

Because your professional hunter will go to great pains to clarify the details of shots to the chest, it seems to me that this discussion might serve you better if it focused on some of the peculiarities of the chest shots. It's interesting that an organ as large as an elephant's heart seems to migrate with amazing facility through the body, depending upon whom one reads on the subject. Normally, it's represented as lying a good deal higher than it really does, perhaps because hunters who have whacked open dead jumbos to confirm the heart's location tend to forget that it will slide upward in the body of an elephant on its side, whereas simple gravity holds it lower under upright, normal conditions. I would, in a straight side approach, place the heart itself at about the level of the base of the ear, from a straight angle partially obscured by the rear portion of the foreleg. However, unless you're shooting a Baker Special or other very large bore, there's no doubt that it is far more effective to place the bullet—especially a relatively small bore—just *over* that organ than it is through it. The reason for this unusual placement involves the simple mechanics of the heart shot. A jumbo's pump is rather like smoked India rubber in texture, tough and springy, and it has a habit of closing up its tissue over a less than fist-sized hole. Because of this, many elephants have been reliably recorded as having lived for hours and traveled miles after what an autopsy proved was a clean heart shot. Yet the big arteries that lead into and out of the heart are not nearly so resistant, and a tusker will usually drop within at most a hundred yards if shot there. The lungs are very large and also effective targets that might be hit if the heart shot is muffed on the high side and doesn't touch the arteries. The lungs are a second choice over the heart, and not as preferable, but if things get fast and spooky, a good hole in the bellows will kill your elephant over a bit of a distance.

Regarding any of these shots, let me howl one major rule: If you stick an elephant with a bullet and he doesn't instantly collapse—don't fret, he won't anyway with chest shots—for heaven's sake swat him again! And again, if necessary. If you or your bullet has screwed up the first try, you may have to walk your legs off to the knees before you have a chance to rectify what you might have done immediately after the first shot. If he's heart- or lung-shot, another slug in the same place will put him down a lot quicker and possibly prevent him from dying in a river or in an area that is nearby but outside the hunting concession. A professional pal of mine had this happen once, and I think the bloody bull is still lying about thirty yards inside a reserve, although shot more than a mile away. The red tape required to prove that he had been initially shot on fair ground and then retreated into the sanctuary was impossible! So if you decide to kill a good bull, for both his sake and yours put him down and keep him down.

Neck shots on elephant are highly academic items I've heard discussed by pros and amateurs alike. I've never tried one so can hardly be an authority. Personally, I could never see the use of such a choice of shot, as the brain, heart, and lungs are all generally available if the neck is. I'm sure that a well-placed neck bullet would be quite effective, but it seems to me sort of lily gilding, although each to his own.

I can't see any place here for a discussion of the hip or spine shots as they are generally, but by no means always, unsporting. The hip shot is normally limited to the professional, used to anchor a jumbo under unpleasant circumstances when necessary, usually when he's retreating wounded. It's very effective if you know what you're doing but strictly a last resort for the sport hunter. In any case, it's used only to stop an escaping animal for the couple of seconds required to run around him and put him down with a side or frontal brain shot.

Some old books refer to the knee or leg shot, which I find unnecessary. In truth, I have never known anybody who ever claimed to have purposely shot an elephant in the leg or knee, and I frankly question whether such a shot is effective. One sees circus elephants doing all sorts of tricks on three or even two legs, so perhaps the old idea that the jumbo needs all four legs isn't true. For sure, I'll never find out. . . .

Obviously, it is impossible in a single chapter to cover more than a fraction of all that elephant hunting entails; even whole books have hardly gouged a furrow in such a fertile field. There are, though, some matters pertaining to jumbos that have caught my fancy over years of hunting and research that seem appropriate for inclusion here.

With all the accumulated folderol over light versus heavy calibers, one shot fired by professional ivory hunter Frederick G. Banks that probably brought more ivory to the auction floor than any other is instructive. Although almost stone deaf—he was known as "Deaf" Banks—he favored the teensy .256 Mannlicher for open shots rather than the .577 he used in cover, as did so many of his contemporaries. In, if I recall correctly, Kenya, he once killed a jumbo on the steep side of a hill. It collapsed and began to roll down the slope, picking up momentum as it went. Turning into an animal avalanche, the body slammed into two more bulls below it, also setting them in cartwheels that ended with all three dead below. I suspect that it would take some doing to beat killing three tuskers with one .256 bullet!

Perhaps not quite so fantastic a feat of luck but certainly one of skill was William Finaughty's killing of six elephants one day in the late 1860s with only five bullets from his heavy muzzle loader. Cutting fresh spoor, he discovered that he had one bullet in his rifle and only four more in his pouch. Killing a cow at first, he galloped his horse after the bulls of the small herd and was nearly killed, barely saving his life by cooling a male in ambush from only four yards, the rifle not even to his shoulder. As Finaughty later wrote:

> Upon looking him over I noticed a curious little knob on his shoulder and pulling out my knife, I cut a slit in the hide and there I found my bullet as perfect as when it was moulded. Firing at such close quarters it had passed through the elephant and nearly out the other side.

With this recovered ball, Finaughty killed another bull and finished the day with a total of six for six shots and only five bullets. That's pretty fair shooting with an old "roer" frontloader.

Whenever talk of elephant starts to swirl around with the campfire smoke, the matter of ivory is usually the first topic to arise. Who killed the biggest elephant in terms of tusks, and when and where? Well, that's an interesting question. The biggest set of tusks ever collected by a white man was taken in the eastern Congo by Major P. H. G. Powell-Cotton, tipping in at a fresh weight of 198 and 174 pounds. The major, unfortunately, didn't match the acquisition of his great trophy with a classic shooting performance, having to belt the blighter eight times with his .400 double rifle, starting with three attempts at brain shots at eighty yards! Interestingly, the *longest* tusks ever taken were not recorded as to origin but in the early 1930s were the property of the Powell-Cotton Museum and are now in the United States National Collection at the Bronx Zoo. They are 11 feet 5 inches and 11 feet even in length and *total,* according to the Tenth Edition of *Rowland Ward's,* 293 pounds. Incidentally, the old record of body size (height at shoulder), which had held for almost twenty years, was upped in 1974 to an unbelievable 13 feet 8 inches with a kill in Angola by E. M. Nielsen, Jr. This beat by a clear six inches the record of Fenykoevi, whose bull stands in the Smithsonian Institution in Washington, D.C. Before moving on to the really juicy stuff, it's only fair to mention that ivory hunter Marcus Daly, whose influence had put the famous Jim Sutherland on the ivory trail professionally, claimed to have shot a magnificent tusker in the French Congo in 1929 that packed teeth of 207 and 203 pounds! Daly said that he sold the ivory to a Portuguese for fifty thousand francs. Personally, despite the rather flamboyant and jealous personality that Daly is reported to have displayed, I'm inclined to believe it. After all, professional elephant hunters couldn't have cared a hoot about sportsman's records; they hunted for a living. Further, it's almost a certainty that at least a few bulls as good or better than the weight record have been taken by poachers and cut into the usual 3-foot commercial lengths so much more convenient to hand carry from "the blue" to the auction floor in Mombasa and elsewhere.

I have been hunting the world-record tusker for more than seventeen years. I've even caught up with him a couple of times, so close that I literally touched him! But to me the completely fascinating thing about him is that he's wound in a shroud of the murkiest mystery. We know where he is and how much he weighs, but we don't know for remotely sure who killed him, how and when and under what circumstances. We don't even know if he should be called "him" or "them." In my mind, though, he'll always be The Kilimanjaro Elephant, the greatest trophy any hunter ever took.

He looms through the legends that are the old Africa, a dim, shadowy bulk like a great gray warship seen through foggy dawn. Others besides me have followed him along the twisting trail of time, but even the cleverest have failed to unravel the enigma of the greatest tusker that ever lived.

He must have been the trickiest and most intelligent of his sage species, for he survived to grow the heaviest of all recorded African ivory. The incredible tusks, which span nearly twenty-one feet when laid end to end, are the most poorly documented of the world's great hunting trophies. There are half a dozen different tales of the ivory's origin and twice that number of "authentic" versions of their individual weights. What is the true story of the Kilimanjaro Elephant, and how heavy was his ivory? Who, if anyone, killed him? It took me nearly ten years to answer these questions to my satisfaction.

I first cut his spoor in a logical place—*Rowland Ward's Records of Big Game*—when I was starting my career as a professional hunter in central Africa. *Ward's* is the reliquary in which most African game trophies are enshrined. The book merely stated that the tusks weighed 226 and 214 pounds and that they were 10 feet 2½ inches and 10 feet 5½ inches in length with girths of 24¼ inches and 23½ inches. Since a bull with tusks of even 100 pounds each is rarer than true love, a behemoth the size of the Kilimanjaro jumbo is the equivalent of a 40-pound largemouth bass or a whitetail deer with 40 long points on each side.

134

If the chaps at *Rowland Ward's* said the record weights were 226 and 214, it was fine with me. Then I visited the Museum of Natural History in London and goggled at the tremendous tusks in their basement chamber. You have no idea what two 10-foot-plus ivory tusks look like unless you see them in person.

One of the museum staffers gave me a copy of a report done by J. E. Hill in 1957 that sets forth the semiofficial history of the tusks and the great bull to which they belonged. While doing research for my first book, *Death in the Long Grass,* some very annoying inconsistencies regarding the tusks popped up when I consulted other authorities. I wanted to mention the ivories in my book and give as much detail as possible about them, but the more sources I read, the greater my confusion became. Nobody seemed to agree on any point—the weight of the tusks, their origin, whether they were found or the bull was killed deliberately, or even if the tusks came from the same animal.

J. E. Hill of the museum's Department of Zoology wrote that the tusks weighed 226½ and 214 pounds. Yet in his classic book, *Elephant,* Commander David Enderby Blunt lists the tusks as 236 and 225 pounds. Further, the caption of a picture in his 1933 work transposes the last digits, which makes one wonder whether the caption is correct and the text wrong. Blunt's measurements also differ slightly from Hill's, enough to suggest that they are speaking of different tusks. Surely, the Department of Zoology of the British Museum could not be wrong, but Blunt couldn't be shrugged off either. His information came directly from a principal official of a company that had owned the smaller tusk.

Denis D. Lyell, who put together a fascinating book called *African Adventure* that records his correspondence with such classic African hunters as Selous, Stigand, Cuninghame, Percival, Hunter, Millais, and a dozen others, also made some references to the record tusks, having become interested in them after purchasing a photographic enlargement of a picture of them in 1907. Noticing a letter from a Mr. V. Myers in the March 16th, 1933, edition of *East Africa*, Lyell wrote to Myers requesting a description and an opinion as to whether or not the two tusks were from the same elephant.

Precisely who Myers was remains unclear to me, for his address differs from that of either company that at one time or another owned the smaller tusk, that is, Landsberger, Humble & Company or the well-known cutlery outfit of Joseph Rodgers & Sons, Ltd., in Sheffield. He may, however, have been with Wolstenholme, Ltd., who acquired the tusk briefly in 1932. However, I will quote Myers' answer to Lyell:

> March 17, 1932
>
> I am obliged for your letter of the 16th, which I find most interesting. The tusk you mention is the one in question, and although it has always been described as forming a pair to the one in the Natural History Museum, it is not, as you surmise, the fellow tusk.
>
> I am of the same opinion as you that both these tusks have shrunk in weight on account of drying.
>
> The one that we have weighs 214 lbs., and the length including curve is 10 ft. 5½ ins., length of hollow part 29¼ ins. The girth at the hollow end, 3 ins. from end of the tusk, is 23 ins.
>
> If you would care to see this tusk, it is at present lying with Messrs. Rowland Ward, Ltd., 'The Jungle,' 167, Piccadilly, W.I. although it is still our property. . . . [Signed] V. Myers.

Perhaps a couple of discrepancies might be understood but from here on things really get sticky. The respected zoologist and naturalist Ivan T. Sanderson produced a definitive book on elephants in 1962 entitled *The Dynasty of Abu.* Sanderson, probably confronted with the same inconsistencies that I found, further muddied the water by writing that the tusks in London numbered *four:* a set weighing a total of 440 pounds—which tallies closely enough with Hill to be unmistakable—and a completely different pair specifically stated to come from the "Kilimanjaro Elephant" that totaled 460 pounds—only one pound away from Blunt's figures. How many first-place world-record elephants could there be?

T. Murray Smith, a founder of the East African Professional Hunters Association, reported in his biography that the biggest tusks ever recorded weighed 236 and 226 pounds and that they were presented to the sultan of Zanzibar and ended up in America! These were obviously not the tusks in London, although he did say that they were from the slopes of Mt. Kilimanjaro. Or was he simply mistaken about their origin?

In a lecture entitled "The Story of the Elephant" given by R. J. Cuninghame, on March 4, 1921, Cuninghame also confuses the fact that one of the tusks was purchased by an American firm with the presumption that it ended up in America. Cuninghame says:

> This elephant was actually shot by a very much underclothed nigger [sic], with a Tower of London musket, that he had stolen from the Germans in German East Africa.

One of these tusks is now in the British Museum, London, and its fellow was purchased by America.

As if the matter weren't sufficiently muddled, the fine contemporary writer Erwin A. Bauer must have been as dizzy from his research when preparing his book, *Treasury of Big Game Animals,* as I was when working on mine. He wrote:

> The largest known single tusk weighed 237 pounds and came from a bull shot in 1899 in Kilimanjaro. The next heaviest tusk, from an animal shot in Kenya [Kilimanjaro is in Tanzania], weighs 226 pounds and measures slightly more than 10 feet long. The opposite tusk weighs 214, the two totalling 440. Both are today in the British Museum of Natural History.

So, by Bauer's understanding, and not unreasonably, there are *three* separate great tusks from two different locations! It's impossible to say where he got the date 1899 for the biggest tusk, which if accurate would rule out the Kilimanjaro Elephant because his ivory is documented as having been photographed and sold in Zanzibar a full year earlier. Still, it was a fascinating idea. *Were* there two separate tuskers, one from Kilimanjaro and another from Kenya? Whom should I believe? Guys like Blunt, Sanderson, Lyell, and Bauer are certainly not casual about facts, and what about the museum?

A lot more than the discrepancies in weight bothered me, and the itch to really determine the true story of the magnificent tusks kept gnawing away at me. Commander Blunt, for example, says the ivory was ". . . supposed to have been found near Mt. Kilimanjaro." Carey Keates of Holland & Holland said in a letter to me that the tusks had been "found," there being no record of whether the bull had been killed or had died a natural death. Hill, writing for the museum, stated that the ivory was taken by a hunter: "It is said that they came from an elephant killed near Kilimanjaro by an Arab hunter after he had been trailing it for several weeks." Sanderson simply declares that the bull was killed on the mountain but not by whom. He also offers the tidbit that the body size of the tusker was not large, but there's no place I know of where he could have read this reliably. Smith told his biographer, Alan Wykes, that the elephant was shot by a ". . . native hunter who used an old muzzle-loading rifle." A current book by a Spanish professional hunter and writer claims that there were also two separate elephants, the biggest a single-tusker, killed by an Arab hunter, whose tooth weighed 235 pounds when taken in 1899, and a *pair* of tusks now in the British Museum, which weighed 235 and 226 pounds fresh. According to the Spaniard, the tusker was taken by an Arab hunter named Senoussi who worked for the slave trader Tippoo Tib, also on Mt. Kilimanjaro. Where the name Senoussi came from I can't imagine but it must be a common source that has eluded me, because I have seen it before. In any case, thanks a lot, fellows!

Then there was doubt about whether the tusks came from the same animal. Lyell, Blunt, and Myers wrote that this was unlikely but Hill states that they indeed are a pair. True, the tusks are not particularly well matched, but then few large pairs are. The shorter and heavier tusk was probably the working tusk, favored by the bull over the other for stripping bark, digging, and other feeding activity. For my money, they are a pair. The color and texture make it apparent that they had been mates in life. At least I had reached one conclusion. Then came a big breakthrough.

I had been rapidly approaching financial oblivion and decided to write another book. One of the more fascinating characters this tome deals with is the amazing W. D. M. (Karamojo) Bell, the Scottish elephant hunter who *walked* more than sixty thousand African miles while hunting ivory. This figure was reached by the peripatetic hunter well before the end of his career. Bell's memoirs were assembled after his death by his friend, the American writer and cartridge innovator Colonel Townsend Whelen, and were entitled *Bell of Africa*. That book offers the only clear contemporary reference to the Kilimanjaro Elephant. I had missed it when researching my first book. Oddly, nobody I have read has quoted Bell on this matter either. Bell sheds a ray of purest sunlight on the mystery.

When Karamojo Bell hunted his way to the slaving village of Mani-Mani in Uganda in 1902, he met one of the most fabulous and infamous leaders of the black ivory trade, a mountain of muscle named Shundi. He was the leader of a less-than-sociable collection of Persian, Swahili, Baluchi, and Arab traders. Shundi's background was as interesting as his occupation was bloody. Born a Kavirondo tribesman, he was himself sold into slavery after being captured as a child by Arabs, but he had the smarts to convert to Islam. The Koran forbids any believer to hold another in slavery. After he attained freedom, he rose within a few years to the top of the business he knew best.

During a conversation with Bell, Shundi told the story of the Kilimanjaro Elephant's death. The great bull had been shot with a muzzle loader, Shundi told

Bell, by one of the trader's slaves, a Chaga tribesman. Stumbling into the elephant by accident practically in the Chaga's backyard on Kilimanjaro near dusk, the slave had fired for the chest. Then he had dropped his gun and run for his life. The next morning, the bull was found nearby, dead as the good old days. As the hunter was himself Shundi's property, the ivory also belonged to the slaver, who had the tusks sent by slave-trade caravan down to Zanzibar, where they were sold in 1898.

Shundi had a sense of humor. He made himself the butt of the story by telling Bell that he sold the tusks for their weight value alone, not realizing that they were worth much more as the largest ever seen. Bell, writing years later, recalled that they weighed 236 and 223 pounds fresh, which is close enough to the early reports on the ivory now in the museum to qualify them as the same pair. Since one of the prime participants in the disposal of the tusks gave this information to Bell only four or five years after the elephant's death, before the ivory had any opportunity to become famous, it has the clear ring of truth. Also, it would have been unlikely for the powerful trader to fabricate a story in which the joke was on him.

Last October, I had another chance to examine the tusks at the Natural History Museum in London and spent quite a while going over them. Having made a living as an elephant hunter myself, I at least knew what to look for. I found much more than I had expected.

Through the courtesy of Dr. Juliet Jewell of the Department of Zoology, I was permitted to handle the tusks and to examine them with a magnifying glass. The evidence rules out the possibility that the ivory was found after the bull had died naturally. The approximate one-third of each tusk that was embedded in the bull's skull and contained the large carrot-shaped nerve pulps bears obvious marks of having been chopped free of the surrounding bone encasing the tusk bases. In fact, the biggest job of dental surgery ever done was a sloppy one. Quite a few pieces were chipped from the ivory with the small ax or heavy bush knife usually employed for the job.

If the bull had been found dead (barring the unlikely event that he was still warm), it would not have been necessary to cut out the tusks. Decomposition of the sockets permits ivory to be pulled out by hand within a few days after death. In such cases, there is no need to risk marring the tusks by chopping. Incidentally, whoever removed them left nearly identical marks on *both* tusks, which indicates that the same person was using the same tool. This reinforces my belief that they are mates. The hunter was inexperienced, in a hurry, or both.

There were still the weight discrepancies to resolve. Nobody seems to have noticed it at the museum, but I found a dim but clearly legible stamp near the base of the bigger tusk, the right one. Dr. Jewell, who had also been unaware of its existence, agreed with me that the stamp, struck with dies like those that proofmark a rifle's chamber, read P454, and directly beneath this cryptic ivory broker's code is the number 237½. Eureka! The tusk listed by the museum as weighing 226½ pounds had *once* weighed 237½ pounds. It was beyond doubt the same one, as Keates had said, but it was lighter because of drying over the years. The left tusk also bore a stamp, but it was not so clear. The dies used were different, and the tusk lacked a merchant's identifying code number. Dr. Jewell and I both interpreted it to *probably* read 226½. This had been the

142

original poundage of the left tusk, now listed at 214. The known history of the ivories themselves, which is well documented after their original sale, seemed to cap off the answer to eight decades of misinformation.

After Shundi's Chaga slave hunter cut out the tusks, they were caravaned east to Zanzibar. An American firm bought them and shipped them to Landsberger, Humble & Company in England, where they were separated. The larger was purchased by the British Museum at an unmentioned date for 350 British pounds. This was quite a bargain. An important point is that Mr. Humble, the dealer himself, who was interviewed by Blunt and supplied the photo of the tusks taken when they were still together in Zanzibar in 1899, clearly asserts that the larger weighed 236 pounds. It had already lost 1½ pounds by the time it reached Britain. Obviously, it had further declined to 226½ by the time the museum had weighed it. Why *Rowland Ward's* does not include the extra half-pound of the larger tusk in its listing is unknown to me.

The smaller left tusk, said by Humble to have weighed 225 pounds, had also lost exactly 1½ pounds by the time of its sale to the famous cutlery firm of Joseph Rodgers and Sons, Ltd., in Sheffield, England. After many years, the tusks were at last reunited. The left one was sold in 1932 to the now-defunct Wolstenholme, Ltd., a company from whom it was acquired for the British Museum through Rowland Ward. If Mr. Myers was a member of Wolstenholme, then his "expert" advice to Lyell was at best third-hand and thus inconclusive.

A 1912 photo of the left tusk in a commemorative booklet by the Rodgers firm clearly shows that it is the same tusk now in the museum. The ivory was on public display until about 1973, when it was removed to the security storage area in the museum's basement, where it is still to be found. The Natural History Museum is most cooperative in arranging a showing for interested sportsmen.

The obvious answer to the mystery seems simple in retrospect. The weights were all correct, or nearly so, but varied according to the date of the source quoted. J. E. Hill, in his (or her) history, was either unaware of the original weights or just plain negligent in not mentioning that they had not always tipped in at the poundage listed. Dr. Jewell didn't think they had been reweighed since coming back together in 1933 (possibly not even then), and if you consider the awkwardness and risk of breakage involved in weighing them, it's clear why. Another source says the modern weight came from a weighing done in the 1960s.

I very much doubt that either is down to the rough 210 pounds guessed at by Carey Keates. Remember, they were 11 pounds apart to start with. After 80-odd years, they are about as cured as they will ever be. There is, however, a fresh crack in the base of the left tusk, which indicates that they are still losing moisture. In any case, their dimensions are as gigantic as ever, and none of the awe I have experienced when seeing them will be lost on you if you find yourself in London. As a hunter, it just wouldn't be right not to pay a courtesy call on the Kilimanjaro Elephant.

5 LEOPARD

HE WAS STILL ALIVE when the men reached my camp on the Munyamadzi River, although I'm sure I don't know why. It was *emeni,* or "midday," in Zambia's dry season, when everything was sensibly quiet in the heat, including me, propped in the cool shade of the sausage tree grove with a sweating Lion Lager in my grubby fist. Things had been thankfully slow in the mayhem department for the last few days, and my game-control duties of shooting raiding elephant or chasing poachers had been light. But there was always the paperwork in quintuplicate, and I had spent the past three days filling in "kill" forms and making the usual inventory of ivory, confiscated poached trophies, and such ready for the official vehicle that would be by any time to pick them up. The three scouts under my command were afield on duty with their bicycles and not due back until the day after tomorrow, leaving in camp only me, old Silent, and a kitchen *toto* to fetch water and wood.

Silent saw them first. Five hundred yards away,

walking across a flat, were two Awiza tribesmen carrying a blanket-wrapped form slung from a pole between them. It didn't take a Sherlock Holmes to figure out what would be in that dirty, torn blanket, either. It looked as if the vacation was over. When they laid it down and unwrapped the tattered edges, even I, who can happily eat my lunch seated on the rapidly rotting carcass of a dead elephant, had to force down a gag. The poor bugger looked as if he'd spent a weekend in a blender set at "cole slaw." Except for the burning, unblinking eyes that stared at me, I would have thought the best medicine for him was a shovel. But he was not only alive, he talked!

The bush African seems to defy most of the rules of modern medicine. You can convince him that he's been hexed, and he'll lie down and die on you in about four days. Yet I've seen him ripped from crotch to clavicle by rhino horn and double-tusked through the intestines by elephant, burned, infected, and shredded by lion, and within a few weeks he's back on his feet again, scarred but healthy despite wounds that would have given a Spanish Inquisitor the queasies. So it seemed to be with this one.

As it happened, despite the fact that quite a lot of his face was hanging free from its moorings, he looked vaguely familiar. When he spoke, I realized that I knew him from the village, for he called me by my African name, Nyalubwe. *Nyalubwe* means "leopard" in Chenyanja, which seemed to throw a macabre humor over the situation. It developed that it had been my namesake that had replatted the man, whose name was Chisi. Silent brought the big medicine kit and had the kitchen lad set water to boiling. We lifted him to the makeshift dining table and, as I listened to him tell his tale, I did what I could to reassemble the jigsaw puzzle of torn flesh.

It had been about an hour after dawn, the sun still low behind the yellow thorn trees, when Chisi had walked from the village with his son, a six-year-old named Ntani, to check his snares for *khwali,* or partridge. Although I of course did not permit the setting of wire snares for game in my area and treated offenders firmly in the extreme, I didn't see much harm in the snaring of an odd francolin or guinea fowl for the family pot, provided only grass cord or light bark fiber was used. At the edge of a grassy *vlei,* dead in the winter dryness, they entered the cover with Chisi leading and carrying his spear. The boy followed close behind.

As I poured disinfectant into one fang hole in his arm and watched it run out another, he went on, his voice oddly calm and clear despite the obvious pain he must have been in since the shock had worn off. At the third snare they visited, a cock guinea fowl was struggling mightily and broke the anchor line just as the pair came up, dashing off still half-tied into the bush. Chisi watched, amused, as the boy chased it through the cover, which was very thick. Then came a shriek cut short, a thrashing, then silence. As quickly as he could run, Chisi bulled through the grass, his spear drawn back for a throw. As he pounded along he almost ran over the grisly scene: a big male leopard standing over his son, whose neck was still in the cat's jaws. So fast that it was a blur, the leopard dropped the child and instantly sprang at Chisi, who managed to thrust at it with the spear blade, missing the chest but cutting deeply into the stomach.

The leopard's lightning charge knocked Chisi down backward, and the cat fastened its long teeth into his arm. The deadly hind legs windmilled, seeking and finding his belly and thighs, flashing claws shredding meat to the bone. A forepaw hooked and held for a

149

moment in the flesh of the right side of his face, pulling the tissue into red ribbons as the claws tore free.

I had just finished stuffing the odd loops of Chisi's guts back into his lower chest and hopefully taping on a sterile, wet compression pack when he finished his story. He had lain for some time, stunned, staring at the lifeless body of his son a few feet away. Already the flies were gathering. Fortunately, the two men who had carried Chisi to my camp had noticed the vultures gathering and gone to investigate, finding him and the boy. They had rigged the *machila* with the blanket and stopped by the village on their way to send a party for Ntani's body.

It was the middle of the afternoon before I had done what I could for Chisi, closing the worst tears with butterfly tape sutures instead of sewing him up, for almost surely infection would develop later. With a butt full of penicillin and a dreamy smile on his face from the injection of morphine, he calmly watched me radio for a Game Department car to pick him up and take him to a small dispensary about fifty miles away that had an Indian doctor. I would have taken him myself, but I had business back in that high grass.

Of the three things I most distinctly dislike doing, digging wounded leopards out of thick bush unquestionably ranks first. In fact, it's my personal belief, based upon experiences I would much rather not have had, that there is no circumstance so potentially lethal in taking any of the Big Five as following up a *wounded* but still active leopard. Because of their size, the big boys—elephant, rhino, and buff—can usually be spotted in time to kill or to turn a charge. Even the lion, although he's more likely to kill you if he can actually close, will betray a charge with a growl or roar, giving you some idea where he's coming from. Not the leopard. He never gives you an edge, saving that rush or spring for such close quarters that he's sure he'll nail you or he won't come. With the most perfect camouflage in nature, he's invisible until he turns into a golden-dappled streak of purest malevolence, biting and clawing with such speed that cases have been recorded in which wounded leopards have been reliably reported as having mauled as many as seven armed men in a single rush and then melted back into the grass before anybody could do anything but bleed.

Once, in Botswana, I tried to force a wounded leopard out of quite a small clump of grassy bush by raking it with No. 6 shotgun pellets. A whole box of shells was used to this purpose. There was never a sound or movement, although I knew I must be hitting the gutshot cat with some of the pellets. Finally, I just had to conclude that it had died of its wounds. But I'd been around long enough trying to keep my lovely profile free of those annoying keloid scars ever to presume anything about leopards. I was as cute entering that grass as a guy on his way to defuse a cobalt bomb. Just as well. Trick or treat. I killed him with a lucky shot at six feet from the hip with a 12-gauge mashie, which didn't do much for his looks. When we unzipped the big tom, we found that he'd collected seventy-seven of those probing pellets from roughly forty yards without a twitch or whimper. My safari client had the ill grace to observe that I had ruined the face of his trophy by shooting it in the chops with a load of buckshot. I don't believe I'll repeat my reply.

Silent and I, guided by the two Awizas, whose names I don't recall, arrived at the *vlei* at half-past four in the afternoon, having left Chisi in the care of the kitchen helper until the Land Rover arrived. I'd done all I could and now the most important matter was to settle accounts with the *Nyalubwe* before somebody inadvertently stumbled into him or he started to develop tendencies toward free enterprise. Man-eating leopards are more rare than lions or crocs with a taste for human flesh, although they often are killers of opportunity, taking a child or woman just as they would any other primate such as a baboon or monkey. Still, from Chisi's account, I think that the leopard merely happened to be in the grass and heard the excited cries of the guinea fowl. As it raced on a collision course with Ntani to catch the bird, the cat probably grabbed the child by reflex as the better meal. Of course, this was mere theory, but as there had been no reports of man-eating leopards in this district for more than a year, I guessed that this was the case. No matter. The cat was wounded and would still chew and claw the Tax Reform Act out of anybody who crossed him and might even turn full man-eater if incapacitated and unable to take his normal smaller prey. Among other things, that's what I got paid to prevent. Helluva way to get rich.

I killed the hunting car's engine two hundred yards from the place indicated by the two men and stepped out, Silent hopping out the rear with my "possible" bag mentioned elsewhere. That there may be no speculation, I am the worst sort of sissy, bearing an ingrained aversion to having my throat torn out, my face pulled off (as happened to old friend Heinz Pullon), or my insides hooked outside by wounded leopards. In anticipation of such occupational hazards, I also keep a few items handy that are sort of alternative contents to the "possible" bag. I think of it as my Black Knight outfit. Not that you'd want to fight the Battle of Hastings in it, but there's a lot of good reasons to insulate yourself as best you can from things that bite. The primary feature is a definitely non–Brooks Brothers leather jacket to which I spent a day riveting big slabs of formica in a flexible pattern. The second item, which would probably get me elected vice president of a New York street gang, is a most fetching antique U.S. Marine leather neck guard originally designed to protect the throat and neck from sword cuts. Not that I don't trust the Marine suppliers of yore, but just to be extra safe, I riveted it over with sheet metal. Somehow, it gives me the appearance of wearing stainless steel dentures. Oh, well, looks aren't everything. I used to have my old football helmet, too, but some tribesman coveted it one dark evening and it is no longer in inventory. Fortunately, I am still on the manifest.

Silent checks out the bag's contents, and you shrug into the jacket, finally lacing up the neck protector. No need for the old .375 H&H; this will be a very personal affair. The Winchester Model 12 slides, silver-worn and sharp with the odor of WD-40, from the soft case. You thumb six rounds into the unplugged magazine, jack one into the chamber, and top off the cargo with a seventh in the magazine. You try not to notice the deep claw marks on the pump's forestock, for they tend to bring up disconcerting memories of similar situations. Unable to think of even the most improbable excuse to stay around the car puttering with your gear, you reluctantly head for the *vlei* and all that bloody grass, feeling much like a gladiator waiting for the main gate to the arena to open. You have decided not to take Silent (who is now pouting) because it's just too thick, and you may have to snapshoot in any direction in a fraction of a second. He would not look very good after a charge of buckshot from a couple of feet and, anyway, good gunbearers are getting hard to find.

The first fifty yards take a full half-hour. The gun is held well back on the hip to prevent the leopard from getting between you and the muzzle. The worn walnut is slippery with sweat. Each step is taken with infinite slowness on the outside edges of the feet. Visibility is down to eight or ten feet, so there's no point in looking for the leopard himself. Instead, you watch for the movement of grass he will be forced to make when he charges. Oh, he'll charge all right, because he's almost certainly still here, lying up and licking his wounds. You follow the trail of Chisi and his son, which blends with the in-and-out bloodstained route of the other men and the party recovering the child's body, until you finally reach the unmistakable place of death. There are large gouts of arterial blood, which means that Ntani bled to death instead of dying of a broken neck. A few feet away there is another patch of torn and red-smeared ground where Chisi was mauled. From the spoor leading away into the grass, it would seem that Chisi may have "washed his spear" well in the leopard, hopefully well enough that he'll be nice and dead, although you somehow doubt it. Well, at least you have something going for you with a blood trail to follow and enough time gone by for the cat's wounds to slow him down. Whoa. Wait a minute. You know better than that. Expect the worst and there'll be no big surprises.

The sun is starting to slip away by the time you find the soggy place in the grass thirty yards from the mauling where the leopard stopped to lie up for a while. Not good. He's moved and you sure don't need shadows on top of everything else. But he's still trickling a thin, crimson spoor on the stalks, so you had better get in gear before you lose the light.

Step. Turn completely around. Listen. Listen hard for the tiniest swish of grass. You've got to know where he's coming from before you can put up that defensive thunderstorm of lead. Twenty more yards. And then you know.

Everything has slowed down except your heart. As if by hypnosis, your eyes are drawn to the grass at your right front. Was there a sound so faint that you didn't consciously register it? Hard as you stare, nothing of the leopard is to be seen. But you're somehow positive he's there, off to the right of the blood spoor, waiting for you on his own track. You can actually feel his eyes through the stems and stalks. Slowly, the shotgun swivels to cover the spot, which looks exactly like every other khaki clump of growth. Sweat is pouring down your face despite the fact that you feel oddly cool. What next?

You don't have to decide. He does. Like an uncoiling steel spring, he's in the air, launched directly at your face, his mask a twisted, befanged horror framed between extended, inward-turned paws that are studded with long, hooked, white claws. Despite his speed, you somehow have time to notice every detail of his awful, sinuous, lithe beauty. Then the Winchester fires—a short, hard bark—and his left front paw disintegrates as the solid charge of shot shreds it on the way to his neck and head. With the trigger still held back, you instantly work the pump. The second swarm of buckshot pours into him as the firing pin slams the primer on the return stroke. A hole the size of your clenched fist appears just where his throat meets his upper chest, visibly slowing him in flight

155

with the terrible impact of the charge. He turns in the air as if somersaulting to crash on his back, as limp as a plastic bag of sausage meat, landing a yard short of your feet with a soggy thump. Without any hesitation, you kill him again. It's a shame to blow such a hole in that beautiful amber and anthracite skin, but you know his will be more easily repaired than your own. Lordie, but a cigarette will taste good with a long swig from the water bag.

You give a sharp whistle and hear Silent fire up the old hunting car as you slip out of the armored jacket and untie the neck protector. In a few minutes, guided by your whistles, the grass is folding down and the hood of the 'Rover pokes its way into view with the snout of a prehistoric, metal hippo. You go through the usual, highly flattering version of what happened for his sake so that he may enjoy the status of having a *bwana* worth lying about. The leopard is easily loaded onto an old piece of canvas and swung over the edge of the pickup tailgate when you happen to notice that your bush shorts are really quite soggy. Must have spilled some water from the jawsack. Yeah.

One feature of the leopard that, if not precisely endearing, at least sets him apart from the other Big Five is that he is reliable. Wound him and you can absolutely count on him to try to bite big chunks out of you, claw you up worse than a bayonet-practice dummy, and throw in disembowelment at no extra charge. It's not very easy to get professional hunters to agree on large amounts of anything, but I hardly know one who wouldn't rank a wounded leopard as the most likely of any critter to charge, and to charge successfully. Because he is by far the smallest of the aggressive game, a few folks don't even rate him in the

Big Five, as I've already mentioned. That shows as much logic as shortchanging Napoleon because he wasn't six feet tall. Some modern historians claim that Attila the Hun was a dwarf! In fact, it's partly the leopard's small size that makes him so terribly dangerous on his terms. He can practically hide in an open-toed beach sandal, his faintest outline veiled by the overdose of vanishing cream provided by his rosetted hide. The big stuff is all fast, but fast is relative, particularly when whatever it is is coming in your direction. Lions are tawny blurs in high gear; buff, rhino, and jumbo all big and seemingly irresistible. Leopards are simply unbelievable.

When things go wrong with a leopard, he will wait until he's pretty well sure of you. By that time, barring a lucky shot and possibly a direct blood relation to Jesus or somebody else with a lot of swat, he'll make a lion's attack seem as graceful as an overweight hound dog puppy's trying to get over a picket fence. Now you don't see him, now you do. Too late, Charlie.

Certainly nothing typical strings one leopard encounter together with another, except perhaps the fact that each is so distinctive. Results—usually the only thing predictable about tangling with *Nyalubwe*—are generally bloody. Just at random, take the experience of a seasoned hunter reported by Dr. Thomas S. Arbuthnot, a prominent American physician and medical professor, while on safari. Arbuthnot's 1954 book, *African Hunt,* should not be confused with the tome of the same name by Colonel Charles Askins, my old friend and hunting companion.

Arbuthnot had killed a lioness after wounding her, a very noisy affair that required four shots, apparently not enough to spook off a leopard that, unnoticed by the doctor, was feeding on a kill on the ground, not twenty feet from where the lioness had passed. Matters become a touch suspicious to me at this point, because although the writer expresses the opinion that the leopard should have been long gone, his professional hunters, Afrikaaner brothers named Carl and Farnie Trichard, believe otherwise. Whatever the case, the Boers were, pardon the expression, painfully correct. Arbuthnot threw a rock into a small patch of grass near the body of the young Thompson's gazelle that the leopard had been lunching upon, and the unwounded tom erupted flat-out in a golden streak straight at Farnie Trichard. Both Farnie and Arbuthnot shot as the cat hung in the air, a dappled javelin, but the lithe form melded with Farnie, giving the hunter a face full of fangs. The left paw reached over the man's shoulder like a display case of linoleum knives while both back legs whirled in a bloody blur that shredded Trichard's lower belly—and you know what's down there. In a struggling, growling, grunting, shouting, screaming mass, they fell to the ground, too wrapped together for any of the men to dare a shot. It is at this exact point in leopard hunting that one would very much like to be back at the New Stanley Long Bar ordering a double vodka gibson, hold the mustard. Unfortunately, a Bloody Mary would be more appropriate.

It was a wonderful collection of arms, legs, paws, tails, spots, and growing crimson. Farnie, with the insane strength of desperation, pulled a reversal that would have won him a couple of points in any wrestling match, let alone one for his life. Flipping the cat over, he got on top. To paraphrase the obvious, however, he had a leopard by the tail and could not let go. Suddenly, as sometimes happens with mauling leopards, the cat figured he had business elsewhere and bolted out from under Trichard. Farnie's brother, Carl, killed it with a grand running shot as Dr. Arbuthnot instantly started stuffing his handkerchief into the facial wounds of the South African. As Arbuthnot wrote:

> Farnie was on his feet with blood streaming down his face. I pressed two folded handkerchiefs indiscriminately into the red smear. They were so rapidly soaked that it was not possible to determine the exact location or the extent of his wounds. . . . While sponging away at his face, a small red circle welled up on the front of his shirt, becoming larger and larger as the blood continued to ooze out of his belly wounds. Blood was also saturating the back of his shirt, torn in shreds where the animal had grabbed him between the shoulder blades. Thinking that the bleeding and general shock were enough to cause most men to faint, I urged Farnie to lie down. He refused, but said rather excitedly, "I must get back to camp—leopard cuts are bad."

Aware of the almost certain infection from the claws and teeth, Dr. Arbuthnot fixed up the camp dining tent as an operating theater. Having done his best to disinfect the whole mess with a potassium permanganate solution ten times stronger than normal, the doctor listed Farnie's wounds, all received in a few seconds:

> Face—bite wounds, particularly on the left side under the eye; there were tooth marks in five places, some of them an inch in length, but all more or less superficial. Left side of chest bitten

and clawed, nipple swollen; some claw marks below nipple. Left arm showed claw wounds on shoulder, middle of biceps, and at elbow. Abdomen—wounds where the hind claws had ripped in, perhaps on the original impact. Back—wounds over and below right shoulder blade, where the animal had fastened its claws when it curled its right paw around Farnie's neck. All wounds seemed superficial, even where flaps of skin and underlying tissues were elevated.

They may have seemed superficial to Dr. Arbuthnot, as compared with perhaps an axe murder, but they nearly killed Farnie Trichard. Infection from the leopard's claws and teeth lowered his body resistance, and he suffered a massive attack of previously dormant malaria. Ten hours after the mauling, the man had a temperature of 104.1 degrees Fahrenheit and, had it not been for the fact that his client was a skilled physician, might not have made it. As things later turned out, Arbuthnot, who thought he had missed the charging leopard, had in fact caught it with a bullet in the right side. Perhaps it was the difference that added up to Farnie Trichard's life.

Frank Miller, a professional of excellent reputation who used to operate in what is now Tanzania back in the 1960s, was also fortunate to have a doctor along when he got his dose of leopard. Following up the wounded *Chui,* as he's called in KiSwahili, Frank missed the cat cold in thick bush as it charged, and then guess whose turn it was. Miller gave the leopard his left arm as an *hors d'oeuvre* and actually managed to boot it off his guts while the leopard was attempting to unzip the hunter. The doctor client, standing nearby in hope of a shot, watched the cat bounce back and remove most of Miller's scalp before it was killed by a second client. The doctor sewed the scalp back so that nobody would know but Frank's barber. Lucky man, Miller.

Dave Ommanney, who was "Our Man in Africa" for the big advertising campaign running back in the days when I worked for Winchester, is hardly unique for the lacing he took from a wounded leopard. Gut-shot by a shotgun slug from his European client, who wisely wanted nothing, whatever, nohow to do with the wounded cat, the leopard slunk into the thick crud of the Ugandan bushveld. Dave went in after it with a double 12-gauge and buckshot and after about a half-hour, Point A met Point B with results that are as frequent as the exception. With a very young Kamba gunbearer along, Ommanney stalked past the waiting cat, and it nailed him from behind, giving the hunter what healed into a topographical map of the drainage system of the Congo Basin between the back of his neck and his tailbone. It also chewed his right arm into the first stages of a chili recipe. The boy gunbearer, however, wasn't the windy type and threw himself on the leopard with a skinning knife despite the fact that the cat had ripped off the kid's scalp so that it hung down over his eyes in a blinding sheet of blood, a woolly wet beret that had been knocked askew.

The young Kamba stuck with it, though, stabbing the leopard until it was distracted from Ommanney. Dave grabbed the shotgun that had been knocked out of his hands and blew the leopard's head into sausage stuffing. Needless to say, the kid became Dave's head gunbearer and presumably lived happily ever after, or at least until 1973 when Kenya closed hunting because all those blood-sport tourists paying the big fees got in the poachers' way.

*   *   *

As thin-skinned, lightly boned animals, leopards don't require the advanced persuasion of the big express rifles, provided a fair, unobstructed shot can be taken. Probably half my clients have taken their *Nyalubwe* with .30 caliber stuff of one flavor or another, the .300 Winchester Magnum being a very effective choice. As we'll soon see, most shots at leopard are "designed" to avoid branches and leaves that might upset a light bullet, and, although plenty have been killed with the .243 and other 6-mm rounds, I personally prefer my people to use the .375. The reason is that nothing is ever quite pat in leopard hunting, and an exit hole from a bigger bullet such as the .375 can save a hunter's life by permitting the animal to check out through blood loss before it has a chance to ambush a follow-up idiot like me. Paul Nielssen, whose camp I took over in the Luangwa when he was badly chewed up by a lion, liked his clients to perforate their leopards with the .458 Winchester Mag with a 500-grain solid! I don't think Paul ever lost one, either. Well, I guess the holes were nice and neat!

The accepted antidote for wounded leopards in dense bush is either to have a sudden call to join the clergy, preferably in an area as leopard-free as the Scottish Highlands, or to break out the shotgun. A quick look at the circumstances of most wounded leopard scenarios will indicate why the scatter-gun is preferred.

Leopards charge from close quarters—twenty yards would be practically a marathon. They're virtually invisible until about a foot from the bridge of your nose and although about the weight of a reasonable chorus girl, actually require more pummeling to stop than the average bull elephant. Yes, a big, well-placed bullet will cool them down considerably, but the real brakes are best applied with a solid swarm of buckshot, the practicality of which is more than theoretical. Let's now turn to the Applied Buckshot Department, and I'll show you what I mean.

The choice of gun and load a professional hunter elects to use is not a trivial one, as the wrong guess can turn you in amazingly short order into something that would clog a disposal. Many pros, being of British persuasion, favor the twin tubes of a double-barreled side-by-side 12-gauge, which isn't bad for starters. If you want to get really *pukka* about the whole thing, the usual choice of shells would be Eley or Kynoch SSG, the English designation for .25 caliber shot that would equate with the obsolete American No. 3 buckshot. Should you wish to firmly establish Living Legend status, your shells will be in the old military brass instead of paper cases, an innovation now ancient, for modern shotshell cases are of plastic and don't scuff or swell when wet, which was what the brass was supposed to avoid in the first place. Americans, who as a group shoot one hell of a lot of buckshot in the course of a year back home, traditionally have a love affair with "double oh," which is supposed to solve absolutely any problems from prowlers to revenuers right quick. And it will, too. But with reservations. . . .

Back in November of 1976, I was tapped by Howard French, editor of *Guns & Ammo*, to run along like a good boy and write something creative about the subtle subject of buckshot. Besides the acquisition of a lump on the right side of my face that looked as if I'd had a Matabele crew whack out my wisdoms, a shoulder so thumped that it looked like a bad painting of thunderstorms over the Everglades, and a week-long headache, I did come away from my buckshot tests with some interesting data.

Essentially, I found that for *dangerous* thin-skinned

game, the stuff is no bloody good past thirty yards, and that's only if you're desperate. On the other hand, within ten or twenty yards, I'd rather have a couple of barrels of buck on my team than any six assorted saints you can think of.

It was a hot day when I conducted the tests, using a fourteen- by fourteen-inch standard paper 100-yard rifle target with an 8-inch bull, lithoed in black. My logic was that eight inches is about the size of the lethal zone of most deer-sized animals and that would happily include such exotics as leopards. I fired something over one hundred rounds, in cold blood from a rest, from distances between ten and sixty yards, using every commercial load from the lightest 12-gauge, to 12-Magnum and 3-inch 12-bore Magnum. The recoil beat me half to death in the light shirt I was wearing until I at last quit with a nosebleed and bells chiming in my ears like Christmas Mass at Notre Dame.

To paraphrase the little girl's classic comments in her book review about penguins, I don't want to tell you more about buckshot than you want to know. However, I would like to mention one very important factor in choosing a buckshot load for dangerous game, and that concerns shot size selection. Most people would automatically pick 00 buck simply because it's so well known through TV westerns. In fact, the 12-pellet 12-gauge "baby magnum" load of 00 is considerably inferior to the same maximum powder loading of smaller No. 1 buckshot in the same shell. The difference lies in the simple and astonishingly obvious fact that at .33 caliber, 00 buck is so large in the shell that there is much wasted space that could otherwise be filled with lead if the bearing surfaces of the big, round pellets didn't have to come into contact with each other. But they must. No. 1 buck is .30 caliber, only ten percent less in diameter than 00 buck and but thirteen grains per pellet lighter. However, because of the way the pellet mass fits into the shotshell, the same shell can fire an incredible seventy-five percent *more* pellets than the Magnum 00 load! What this means is that when you need help in a big way, you're launching eight hundred grains of lead at better than three thousand foot-pounds at the muzzle with No. 1 buck compared with a bit over six hundred grains and not quite twenty-four hundred foot-pounds with the 00 buck. If you don't reckon that can make a significant difference, you've never had something try to eat you.

One might also bear in mind that eight hundred grains of lead in a swarm has the individual pellet impact area of an umbrella, for even though still in a solid mass at more or less ten yards, it covers a circular saturation point of about a 7-inch circle. Eight hundred grains, remember, equals a .458 *plus* a .375 at point blank, and you've got two barrels of the stuff, minimum.

The important thing to remember about buckshot is that it disperses in a geometric pattern that would give a computer short circuits if it had to figure out the loss of effectiveness past very close range. The pellets are round, ballistically speaking about the worst shape for a projectile, and the penetration of the lead shot is—as my bushier friends would say—bugger-all beyond about forty yards.

When I was hunting with George Lenher, who took a record-book leopard some years ago, I had a chance to see how ineffective buckshot was at even moderate ranges. We were up along the Munyamadzi wondering what God was smoking to produce a sunset like the one that enshrined the bait, half an impala in a sausage tree about forty yards away from the blind, when a real lunker of a tom suddenly appeared on the bait branch. I nudged George, who smoothly settled into the stock of his .404 Jeffery, lined up the scope, and blew a 400-grain soft-point at the leopard that passed through it and rattled among the trees beyond. This is the only time I've ever seen such a hit not kill the animal instantly. We watched in surprise as it stiffened, dug in its claws, and stayed right where it was. I remember telling George to give the damned thing another dose just above the waterline when it half-jumped and half-fell out of the *muSassa* tree and started off for some thinnish woods nearby. I carried a Beretta over/under 12-gauge in those days, stoked to the tonsils with SSG, about the equivalent of 00. As the leopard disappeared into the shadows, I gave it both barrels, and I know I was holding dead on. I, who normally carry enough ammo to provide a dove hunt for the Mexican Army, was now out of shells for the shotgun. Don't ask me why. Put it down to lack of ethnic understanding. Instead of my usual arsenal, when I opened the "possible" bag, I saw a double brick of .22 rimfire. I took George's .404, despite the scope, and went in, ecstatic to find the leopard *hors de combat* from the first shot and not hyped to damage Zambian-American relations. I'm not sure if I waited for him to die or shot him again. I don't remember, but I'd guess the latter.

When the cat was skinned out, three of those shot-shell pellets were discovered; one actually hung out of the skin and popped free with a pinch by Silent. For sure, they did it not the slightest harm at that range. On the other hand, should you be sneering at the horrendous crunching power of the shotgun up close and personal, let me report that the head of a lioness that had been crippled by a broken wire snare and had charged me when I was bird hunting with light No. 7½ or No.8 shot, a bit puny even for guinea fowl, looked like a melon somebody had backed over after I pasted her at halitosis distance.

I really don't know. Maybe the answer is the "drilling," a popular continental European combination gun with one or another mixture of a pair of shotgun barrels and a rifle barrel nested in between. The only problem is that one usually has to operate a selector button to decide which barrel will fire, and it would just be my luck to have it in the wrong position. Murphy, of Murphy's Law fame, is a devotee of leopard hunting, always happy to prove the point that anything that can go wrong will, and at the worst possible time. Murphy purely loves leopards.

Since my little Beretta over/under was stolen, I have switched to the Model 12 Winchester pump gun, the old model that lets you fire by holding back the trigger and slamming the slide home with the firing pin depressed. It holds seven rounds, which is, let's see, fifty-six hundred grains of No. 1 buckshot (seven thousand equals a pound), and with a bit of practice it can be used more or less like a fire hose. If you've read some of the earlier books in this series, you will know that it has done wonders for the extension of my literary career.

With leopards, I've always stayed with a full complement of straight buckshot for one easy reason: they don't try to get away when they have something less than a bull's-eye in their guts. Getting close enough for buckshot is, to the fatal discovery of professionals and amateurs alike, not the problem. The dilemma is staying far enough away to kill the bloody things before they can kill you. Of course, buckshot doesn't always work. Sorry I can't use a leopard for the illustration offered by Denis D. Lyell, but I suspect you'll get the idea.

After first pointing out an instance in which an old black woman killed a potential woman-eating lion when it sprang at her by giving it a couple of thousand grains of garden-variety hoe and smashing its skull, Lyell then brings up the matter of SSG British buckshot. I might as well quote him:

> I may say a shotgun, even with heavy shot such as S.S.G., is not much use against a lion, unless at a range of less than a dozen yards or so. [Apparently, he found the same thing I did.]
>
> I once saw the skin and skull of a large lion shot by a youth, Monty Foord, the son of Mr. J. A. Foord, who had a farm near Fort Jameson at that time. [Fort Jameson is now Chipata, in Zambia, my old headquarters.] He had disabled the lion with a .303, fortunately hitting its spine, which paralyzed its hindquarters. He then blazed at it with a 12-bore shotgun and S.S.G. shot at thirty yards, and, running out of cartridges, approached and tried to lay it out with an axe, which was plucky, but rash. Later on he got hold of more rifle cartridges and finished it off.
>
> The skin of the head was full of holes and there were several flattened S.S.G. pellets still sticking in the skin. They had failed to even crack the skull, and none had penetrated, as I examined it carefully.

Young Monty, incidentally, despite his intrepid attempts to ax lions, succumbed to sleeping sickness and died a short time later. Africa has many options for the rash.

To close down on the Buckshot and Lonely Hearts Department, let's just say that, given ranges under twenty yards and preferably half that, the stuff is absolute magic on thin-skinned game. At long range, try praying. It's probably more effective.

Having spent a large wedge of my life hunting the dangerous game of Africa (and elsewhere), I cannot but conclude that the leopard is hands down the slickest. The combination of intellect, natural shyness mixed with incredible boldness when things are going his way, and physical makeup, aggregate a creature that is without equal as an opponent to a sportsman. Should you fall for some of the trash that labels him as endangered, just remember that he's still the most widely distributed of the feline predators, and that for one reason: he's the very best at what he does. Sure, you'll find pumas or mountain lions from Alaska to Patagonia, but they're literally pussycats compared with the leopard. Leopards kill at will, including human prey, from the frozen wastes of Siberia all the way down to South Africa, ranging in habitat from purest tidal swamp to the wind-blasted heights of Kilimanjaro, where Hemingway cryptically noted, "Close to the western summit [of Kilimanjaro; 19,710 feet] is the dried and frozen carcass of a leopard. No one has explained what the leopard was seeking at that altitude."

Leopards, like men, in whose modern presence they exist in a close symbiosis based upon garbage, pet dogs, human corpses, and the all-too-frequent child or woman, are professional adapters. They are survivors. And, like men, they sometimes give way to their excesses.

With the exception of one tigress, the most difficult

of all the man-eaters to kill have been the leopards. Sometimes years are required to sort one out, and killers who have run up totals well into the hundreds aren't all that unusual. The Panar Leopard of India had better than four hundred human kills; in recent years a couple, also in India, have run past one hundred human victims, finally learning to specialize in hunting the hunters by waiting up over the grisly tatters of their last half-eaten kill.

Lions and tigers usually kill and eat men when desperate, or when injured and unable to catch their more common prey. Of course, the end result in both cases is that of extreme hunger, *whatever* the cause. Not leopards. They go on murderous binges, sometimes doing to humans what has become their trademark with livestock.

Constantine J. P. Ionides, the Anglo-Greek game officer who ran what is now the Selous Reserve in Tanzania (then Tanganyika), came across an interesting example of this bloody behavior. Ionides, a hugely talented hunter, noted that the pattern of leopard man-eating was vastly different from that of lions and cited the extended instance of one leopard on the Ruvuma River that killed twenty-six people, mostly women and children, near Masaguru Village. The interesting point is that not one victim was in the least fed upon. There were thoughts that the big cat had been driven off each time it killed a person, but this was later clearly proven untrue. When shot by Brian Nicholson, Ionides' assistant—the same man who went through the Selous with Peter Mathiessen and was featured prominently in his recent book, *Sand Rivers*—the leopard was casually feeding on an elephant carcass. As Ionides wrote, ". . . it was in excellent physical shape; which suggests that at least it had not been driven to killing humans through necessity."

170

In 1940, another fifteen people were bitten through the throats at Isoka in the Luangwa Valley nearly in my backyard. No flesh was eaten, but there was no possibility of ritual murder.

There are hundreds of verified accounts of a night-marauding leopard killing all the goats in a pen but eating little or none of the meat. The famous ivory hunter Jim Sutherland recorded one attack in which a leopard broke into his duck pen and, making thirteen separate trips, bit the heads off his thirteen ducks. All the bodies, uneaten, were found in a small area between the pen and a light patch of nearby bush. Sutherland later managed to kill what was probably the same leopard with the help of his prizewinning bull terrier, Brandy. It was quite a battle, and in itself a rarity in that the dog was able to fasten its teeth into the leopard's neck skin while Sutherland shot the cat. Leopards love killing and eating dogs, and leopards' superior moves in short order make most canines look as if they're soaked in drying glue.

The boldness of leopards, which can be exasperatingly shy under hunting circumstances, is sometimes hard to believe. One young woman, the daughter of a government official living in Nairobi some years ago, opened her bedroom door and saw what she presumed to be one helluva big dog asleep on her bed. She quietly closed the door and advised her father, who went for his gun. As he reopened the door, the "dog" was sitting up and stretching. He shot dead a big male leopard. Something almost identical happened in Nyasaland when a young white girl noticed the tip of a leopard's tail sticking out from under her bed. She called her brother, who dosed the cat with a load of buckshot. I killed one asleep in the blind I had built to ambush it on one safari.

The leopard's love of dog flesh sometimes brings it

into homes and huts as if it owned the place. In proper cities, leopards have walked into cocktail parties and grabbed poodles, and heaven help the dog off his leash in heavy bush. I doubt that even a staghound would be much of a match for a leopard, given the blinding speed and ferocity of the cat. Lions seem a bit perplexed and annoyed by dogs but don't really appear to respect them; thus in the old days many lions were killed with the use of hunting dogs. Some leopards have been taken in this manner, but usually it's the dogs who come out on the short end, if at all.

The point is that the leopard is the single most effective member of the big carnivores. Wild dogs and wolves are high achievers in areas where they haven't been run plumb out of habitat, but then they participate in group, or social, hunting, which cannot be compared with the lone assassin tactics of the leopard. The leopard is, in my opinion, the greatest of the single-hunting mammal predators, a pure sneaking, killing, and eating machine that is equally at home in habitats ranging from the steam-iron heat of below sea level to the snowy, soughing, wind-raped Russian *taiga;* from the sweating, rotting rain forests to the bleak, rocky wilderness of the Himalayas. He is the greatest hunter larger than the shrew; and that's why I so love to hunt *him.*

It is the high intelligence of the leopard as well as his natural stealth and caution that sets the pursuit of the species on a plane of its own. Among the Big Five, the techniques of leopard hunting are unique. Spooring or tracking is impossible—except as proof that a leopard is in the area—as a direct means to an end. The only practical although very difficult method is therefore baiting. Should the person not privileged to have hunted leopard in this manner get the idea that this is something akin to spearing a hunk of cheese on the tang of a rat trap, let's have a closer look at the process.

It is the habit of leopards, upon making a kill, to remove the *corpus delecti* from any spot where it would be noticed by vultures who would perforce attract other meat-eaters. Most people don't realize that lions consider leopards purely delectable and will kill and eat them any time they have a chance, which isn't too often. It's a fundamental facet of their adaptability that leopards will eat damn near anything, including dead meat that would give an experienced graves registration team the dry heaves. This hasn't done wonders for the leopard's public image, but it does show that *Chui* or *Ingwe* or *Nyalubwe* will do what needs to be done to exist. That leopards far prefer fresh meat to carrion doesn't seem to be mentioned very often, true though it be. Actually, leopards live happily on small fish, insects, mice, rats, birds, and such as well as the better fare offered by an area with high antelope populations. They are essential in keeping down the monkey and baboon populations in agricultural regions and really do quite a lot of good, provided the farmer doesn't mind missing a dog or a few chickens from time to time. In more remote African districts, he probably does as much to process unburied human bodies as does the hyena, the jackal, or the lordly lion, which, at least in my observation, has an even less discriminating nose. But in the hunting areas, where leopards primarily feed on smaller antelopes and buck, the classic tactic of hunting the big cats becomes possible: leopard baiting.

On occasion I have heard people who have either never done it or have tried it unsuccessfully call leopard baiting unsporting. That just isn't so. And if you'll add up all the welts, scars, tears, and puncture marks on the majority of professional hunters, I don't think that you'd find many who would go along with that outlook, either.

Leopard hunting is hugely different from the tracking and spooring of jumbo, buff, rhino, and, to a lesser degree, lion. Things are completely reversed, for instead of going to the game, the problem is now to bring the cat to *you* under conditions he finds unnatural.

The best possibility of taking a leopard, provided that he hasn't been shot at before and spooked, is over his own kill. I used to offer the equivalent of a ten dollar reward for any of my men who could spot a natural leopard kill, which was one big chunk of change to a man who lived well on a salary of sixty-five cents a day, plus food and medical care. The idea was to give them an incentive to look at something other than the tops of their feet as we hunted along. It worked fairly well, too, for several leopard larders, each stuffed with the body of a freshly killed and partly eaten antelope or warthog, were found each season. Almost invariably we killed leopard off them, too. The point is that a leopard doesn't tend to be suspicious of a meal he has placed in a tree himself, whereas he will think twice about Greeks (or Americans) bearing gifts.

When a leopard hits pay dirt in hunting, he kills either with a bite to the back of the head or by crushing the throat cartilage. As soon as possible, he will drag off the kill, carrying even very heavy carcasses considerable distances and up trees. Some kills have been weighed at better than three hundred pounds.

The largest example I have ever seen of a leopard kill, one far too heavy to be removed, was in 1981, in

174

a dry riverbed of the Letaba hunting concession in the Transvaal, South Africa. In company with my friend Gerhard Weber and Nick Van Zyl, a local professional, we found an old kudu cow, fully 450 pounds, lying in plain sight on the sandy ground. The spoor showed that it had been killed in short order by a leopardess of about one hundred pounds accompanied by a cub that couldn't have weighed more than forty pounds, thus no help in the assassination. There were numerous bites to the back of the head—female kudu have no horns—that had been fatal. The briskets had been eaten away as neatly as if cut off by a butcher, as was a neat circular portion of the rear end. My best guess was that the deed had been done near dawn the day before we found the kudu and was thus about thirty hours old. Curiously, there were no vultures or hyenas, although the body was plainly in the open. That there had been a record cold spell probably helped keep the scent down, which explained why the hyenas hadn't found it, but why the vultures were nowhere about must have been just bad luck on their part. We took the backstraps and filets with no compunction, although one man stood guard with a rifle just in case mama was lying up close by and took exception.

As we weren't out leopard hunting, we left the kill after taking the choice meat, but I'll bet you that had we left it undisturbed and wanted a leopardess, the old girl would have shown up about dusk, a perfect target against the white sand. Well, that's always the way. As the Englishman said, "The things you see when you don't have a gun." Of course, female leopards are generally not shot by sportsmen any more than are other female animals, especially with young in evidence.

But, okay, enough about the theory of leopard hunting, as skeletal as this offering has been; now let's see how it works under field conditions.

You've already shot a bait, a warthog with a face out of *Star Trek*, a big boar that might weigh in at 175 pounds with worn but even ivory that will grace your bar back home as mug handles or bottle openers. He's got more crawly interior parasites than an Iowa worm farm, so passing up a detailed culinary inspection of his worth produces nothing more than a sigh of relief. Silent whacks off his nose just past those weird warts, and Invisible or Stomach start whittling away the meat to free the tusks. It was a good shot, a tricky two hundred yards as he trotted through a big hole in the low second-growth *mopane,* his image shimmering and dancing through the Weaver cross hairs just ahead of his chest. Then the .300 fired and the hot breeze brought back the soggy thwop! of the bullet. By the time you had pulled the scope down out of recoil and refocused, he was on his side, the slender legs that protruded from the barrel body swishing in the air as if they were going somewhere. The pro grunts approval and the rest of the crew grin with oddly childish delight for those who have seen so much killing. Scratch one *Ngulube.* That's you, boy, indicates Silent, Bwana Knock 'Em Dead. With a grunt, three of the men heave-ho the body into the back of the 'Rover and off you go to the first of the leopard "sets," chosen that morning.

It had taken several hours to pick out the ambushes. The most important ingredient was a proper tree; more, a proper tree in proper cover. Leopards don't tend to dine just anywhere, you have learned, and a tree with plenty of surrounding trash, featuring a nice, easy angle of climb and slathers of grass, low bush, and other lovely stuff a leopard can use to get right up to it without being seen is as essential to the arrangement as shadows to a mugger. It's still near midday, so a reasonable amount of thrashing in the area is permitted. Should a leopard be around, he'll just put it down to the usual antics of those odd, ill-smelling animals on two legs. There's no bait up yet, and so nothing to draw special attraction to the spot in any case.

The story runs through your mind as you feel the mild stirrings of the morning tea, brewed up during a break at ten. Your professional hunter has tactfully warned you to watch your step by relating the Saga of the Unknown Client, a mortifying ballad of simple thoughtlessness.

It was a dream setup, the professional sagely relates, dragging on one of those strange African brand-named cigarettes, his young eyes hooded by years of squinting into the glare, heat, and dust of safari life until the top half of his head looks ten years older than the rest of him. It flits through your mind that the opposite is the case with bonefish and tarpon guides in the Florida Keys, who have odd, two-toned mugs. The leopard, says the *Baas,* was the sort of chap bound to end up in the Smithsonian, if only for size. His spoor showed that he had feet the size of scalloped serving platters, and given the amount of meat he ate from the impala bait the first night, he either kept a pack of pet, tree-climbing jackals or was big enough to snack on rhinos between regular kills. The *Baas* actually *did* hear him crosscutting wood with the harsh rasping call used by male leopards to either advertise through the dark for female companionship or to warn potential poaching males. By God, he *did* sound big, said the *Baas.*

It was then time to set up a new bait since the old

boy was feeding regularly and the hunter didn't want to push him until he'd become all calm and used to his new soup kitchen. The hunting car was loaded with all the camp staff and a fresh impala, plus the client. The cat had practically worn a highway through the bark of the easy side of the tree with his talons and was just about bonded to show up a good half-hour before shooting time expired, thirty minutes past sunset. Everybody was teetering on the brink of fame; the client, the pro, and the staff for the lavish Maharaja-style tips that would surely be distributed by the *Inkosi* upon the demise of such a great cat.

The hunting car had pulled up about three hundred yards from the bait tree, willing hands as calloused as belt sanders grabbed the new impala half, the client took his own rifle, and the hunter slung a shotgun over a sun-bleached khaki shoulder. At the tree, the head tracker unwound the wire of the first bait and the men jointly hoisted the second into position. The Number One gunbearer reinspected the blind and pronounced it perfect, as nefarious as Nefertiti and as quietly unobtrusive as computer fraud. All that was needed was the leopard on the following afternoon and a barn door shot from the client.

As everyone piled back into the vehicle, the client suddenly remembered that he'd left his dark glasses on a stump back near the bait tree. Supercautious, the pro insisted on going with him to retrieve them. The professional paid no attention as the client went past the perfect bait tree that would hold the world-record leopard, scanning instead the minute details of the bush around for something he might have missed. It was too late when he heard the liquid sound. Without a thought, the client had opened his fly, produced his, um, dingamalery, and completely saturated the base of the bait tree. Of course, nothing keeps away wildlife more effectively than to mark territory with urine, and sure enough, it was the case here. *Hlala gahle, Ingwe. Hamba gahle,* leopard. *Kwaheri.* Bye-bye. Now and forever. The professional was still on Valium a year later, he advised you, despite an otherwise well-balanced life, the latter proclamation debatable.

Moral: Do not pee-pee on bait trees.

You scrunch up your guts and watch Invisible scamper up the tree, squatting casually twenty feet off the ground as the professional moves off, standing where the blind will be and lining up the Awiza as if he were the leopard. With the flick of a hand he indicates a few leafy sprigs to be removed until he's satisfied that there is a clear skyline for what may be the shot. Invisible drops them down to Silent, who catches them and sticks them in his waistband. It is apparently suspect to leave torn branches lying around. Half of the warthog, hatcheted in twain, appears from nowhere and is hoisted up by a braided buffalo rawhide rope and held in place until Invisible is able to wire it through the hocks. Invisible, who is built like a mixture of a smokehouse and a safe, seems an odd choice for the high-wire act, but he is clearly at home in the branches. Deftly, he attaches the 80-pound chunk to the bottom of the limb, obviously an awkward spot for the leopard to reach.

As Invisible lithely eases out of the tree, Silent and Stomach are smearing a welter of blood and scraps of offal against the claw-dimpled bark not only to mask their own scent—which the hunter says doesn't matter much—but to give a broader base of windborne odor. Leopards don't smell much better, if as well, as people do and as in politics, every little bit of stink helps. It is now time for the Rural Architecture Department. The blind must be built.

The professional takes great pride in his leopard

blinds, or, as he corrects, "hides." They are at once the most casual-appearing and the most cleverly designed structures used in the hunting of dangerous game. To be "proper"—as apparently everything must be—each must first be an actual part of the landscape, offering no features that are not consistent with the surrounding *miombo*. The blind must not only be inconspicuous to a felony but must also be located just right to outline the bait-feeding cat against the riot of sunset but to remain in shadow itself so as not to catch the glimmer of metal or glass of a scope sight. This one will probably be just right, you are told, gapping the tawniness of a stand of half-crumpled dead grass with the snaggle of a fallen, elephant-killed tree. With the twink! of hard steel *pangas* cutting seasoned deadwood, a small hollow is carved into the fallen treetop, a cavity about five feet by five feet. As the *Baas* explains, it is not meant to accommodate a cocktail ball, but just to give enough space for one of the men to mind the back door as well as permit enough room to swing a rifle if things get defensive.

None of the material for the "hide" is taken from the immediate area for fear that the odor of sap or the flash of a whitely scarred branch slice will give things away. Piece by piece, sheaves of dead grass are brought through the heat from hundreds of yards away and mixed with the dry boughs of the same type of tree that has fallen victim to elephants here and in the distance. You ask Silent what kind of tree it is and receive a series of sounds that resemble a national election among crickets. On the presumption that he understood your question in the first place, you decide to think of it personally as "leopard wood."

Bit by stalk by leaf by bark slab it is not erected, it is assembled. It's possibly the only structure outside of the military that's supposed to look like anything *but* a structure. It sure doesn't, either. When it's finished, you could turn around and forget where you left it. Which is just right. It rather resembles your mother-in-law's taste in Thanksgiving dried arrangements, or your ex-wife's sense of humor. It offers all the shining imagination of a hanging judge with a hangover. But it sure is neat inside. Instant anonymity. There is a teeny three-cornered camp stool, a ragged hole in the plaited side that just admits the height of your rifle with scope, and Silent is playing shop steward by packing in the red earth with the butt of his hatchet around the base of the rear vee-support. Two sticks have been perfectly aligned to hold the .375 so that you won't have to move it to find the *Ingwe* in the sight picture. If he shows up, that is. You hunch down and check the cross hairs through the scope against the half wart-hog, already showing a nice attraction for flies. They are locked solidly about eighteen inches above and slightly toward the base of the tree. Hell, you'll hardly be needed. Or so it seems now.

By an unheard signal, the hunting crew assembles and starts back through the maze of brush, stacking themselves back into the open pickup. Three miles down the faint track of a wet season wash, the exercise is repeated. Now the drill is to hunt elephants far from this area or just hang around camp and wait. At these prices, elephants almost look like a bargain.

Two days pass—without an elephant—before there is a clear sign that a leopard is feeding. "Bloody good news," says the pro. "Usually takes four or five." Finishing a perspiring beer, he crushes the can and leaves it teetering on the table for the kitchen *toto* to collect along with the plates, denuded of cold breast of guinea fowl and buffalo tongue.

181

"Seems that rifle of yours is zeroed, but let's dou-
ble-check that it hasn't caught a small dose of Africa.
We'll try that cat later and I want to be absolutely sure
nobody tried to hammer a nail back into his shoe using
your Weaver as an anvil."

Murphy lurks everywhere, you have seen for yourself. Before dawn, he sneaks in and puts mustard on
the breakfast cereal. He mixes the .375 softs with the
.458 solids. He puts oil in the radiator and water in the
oil sump. Tireless, he swaps the salt for the sugar in
the bowl. He is probably a relative of someone to
whom you owe money. You sure don't want to trust
him around leopards.

"It's exactly forty-one of my paces from the gunport
to the base of the bait tree," confides the *Inkosi*.
"Add three more yards for the height of the bait and
we'll put your scope spot-on." He pauses to light a
cigarette, bursts a big kitchen match into blue life with
a thumbnail dirtier and thicker than a tortoise shell,
and takes a big drag. The incredibly delicious odor of
the sulphurous match tip, followed by the scent of the
Rhodesian blend almost hits you physically. But then
you quit three years ago. Didn't you?

A single whack of the *panga* leaves a palm-sized
blaze of white underwood as Silent steps aside. A
wave from the pro sends him bounding off into the
bush, safe behind a big termite heap. "*Lungile manji,
Bwana,*" sounds his muffled voice. Okay to shoot.
You lean over the folded bush jacket piled atop one of
the removable car seat cushions and find a solid hold.
When the slightest swaying of the body springs dies,
the big post of the lower central cross hair settles dead
on the pale blaze on the tree. The trigger is crisp, the
kick that flares your hair unfelt in your concentration.
Still staring through his binoculars, the pro yells,

"*Hlala, Silenti. Tina zo shaya futi.*" Stay where you are. We're going to shoot again. A drawn-out "*ehhh*" echoes hollowly from the termite hill. For damned sure, that's one old man not about to wander into the line of fire.

"Call that shot, chum," says the pro.

"I make it dead-on but probably high because this howitzer is zeroed for one-fifty," you answer in your saltiest bush talk.

"Give the man a kewpie doll." Another scratch of match. "Bring her down [why are rifles always feminine?], oh, say, six clicks and stick another in there."

You do.

"Let's go leopard hunting," said with what could possibly pass as an undertone of a compliment.

You don't go leopard hunting in the middle of the afternoon, but a short lie-down is in order. The sound of the hot, windblown branches of the *brachystegia* under which your grass *kaia* has been built soon lulls you into a grogginess that passes into sleep. Ten seconds after you've started to snooze, a white rainbow of denture adhesive and teeth looms up and says what must presumably be that you should get up. That you don't speak Fanagalo or Chenyanja or anything less remote than English—which after all is reasonably remote here—seems to slow down communication not in the least. You gratefully slurp the hot tea, laced with sugar and milk, and begin to feel in a mood to take on a leopard. What the hell, make it a dozen.

It's nearly four before the car, loaded with camp staff, starts off for the leopard blind. The sun, still quite high, is starting to drop like an incandescent elevator weight, nestling into the dirty, stained teeth of *Nkulunkulu,* the great God of Creation: snaggled fangs of worn thunder cloud from which mutters and

183

curses emerge, muffled by the distance. Soon it will be the rainy season, cha, cha, cha.

Windmilling from the heat, the engine takes a few seconds to die, at last rattling into stillness. There are eight men besides you, and they walk off, talking loudly, directly toward the blind. You feel an impulse to tell them to shut up but suddenly remember that you're the beginner. They must have done this many times before. "Just ease your tail over by the blind, nice and casuallike, and edge in onto the stool," says the pro in a normal voice. He notices your look of astonishment at all the milling around and talking.

"Leopards are clever as hell, but they're not too sharp on their sums," says the hunter, suspending a double Greener 12-bore over his shoulder by a sling. "You can bet your last traveler's check that he's watching us right now, probably not from very far away, either." The bloodshot eyes scan the heavy tree line, darting and probing. Unseen, the rude voice of a gray lourie, the go-away bird, sounds from the distance, a thin feminine call against the thump of thunder over the valley.

"He'll see all these people wandering around and get confused as to how many there are. When I'm in the blind with you and Silent, the rest will make plenty of racket leaving, and our boy will feel nice and secure again. If anything, I think this performance makes 'em come earlier." He stares hard at the swirl of storm seeming closer and more threatening now. "Let's hope it works today. Me old wounds, all gotten by acts of great glory in The Wars, seem to indicate that it's going to get a mite damp out here."

You lay the .375 into the vee sticks and tap it this way and that with the heel of your hand until the cross hairs, based with the extra-thick post, are just above the vermin-crawling dead pig. Through the lens, a big crater in the fly-swarmed hams shows deeper red, looking almost as if it's covered with some sort of lint. As you look more closely, you see that they are small stringy ligaments that must slip through the cat's teeth when he shears off a chunk of *Ngulube* with the side of his face like a pair of hedge clippers. With the scope variable at full power, individual claw marks and torn bark shreds stand out clearly in the rope of sun stretching from just above the thunderheads.

You wonder what time it is, glancing at the oddly white band around the pro's wrist. Both watches are back in the vehicle, one on each of Invisible's wrists. Should the leopard come from the rear and pass very close by the blind, he would probably hear them ticking, says the pro. The ones that use batteries and hum are pure poison, he advises. Cost him a very big *Nyalubwe* once. He says something—half-heard—about goddam modern technology.

The little reef of bush seems to be coming to life, the fork-tailed fly-catching drongos flitting above the ground and the dull, whitish, looping clumsiness of lesser hornbills showing through the distant trees. You wish now that you had drunk some water but forget it as the mixture of pain and numbness spreads out through your bottom. Who would have believed that lousy canvas could be so hard? Inch by inch, you shift, drawing what is not quite a glare from your hunter. Through a tiny gap in the blind—you mean "hide"— you see a pair of red-necked francolin toddle by in their odd, top-heavy manner. They clear the gunport by ten feet and all let a held breath escape. Had they flushed, it would have queered the deal. The leopard is out there, you can bloody well feel his eyes probing the bait area. *Bloody well?* Hell, he's got you talking like him now!

The storm begins with a wave of chill wind, so much

cooler than the usual heavy humidity of late October that it's refreshing as a cold shower even though the air is charged with more than thunder. A verbit monkey chatters a hundred yards away and you can feel the hunter stiffen, his head cocking slightly. Five seconds later, a chorus of shrieks rips through the bush and the sun-faded eyes turn on you. An imperceptible nod of the head tells you more than a paragraph. The troop of monkeys has spotted the leopard, past the bait tree and to the left. He's coming.

A complete migration of whooping cranes takes flight in your stomach, sweat springing out through the light khaki of your shirt and speckling it gray. It's harder to breathe. The colors, a moment ago dull, dead, and dun, now seem brighter. The checkering on the Remington's grip is sharper than diamonds under your clammy paw. Slowly, slowly the little binoculars are raised to the hunter's stubbled face and he locks them to the bones supporting his bleached eyebrows. Forever, he stares out a fist-sized hole on his side, combing each cowlick of grass, peering into each tiny islet of bush. You involuntarily start as a clap of thunder crashes with a savage, orange-blue lash across the blackening sky ahead. You keep your eye to the scope, cursing your thoughtlessness in having turned the lens up to eight-power. There's almost no field of view, just big chunks of very dead warthog and pieces of tree limb. You know better than to move to try to crank it down to 3x or 4x, though. Well, the better to see you with, my dear.

The touch on your leg almost shocks you through the side of the "hide." A hairy mitt nudges your thigh as the hunter signals that he's here. *Here?* Here. *Where,* for Christ's sake?

The light is as diffused as a bad bruise, gray and

sickly orange with an overcast of decaying gangrene green. Moving less than an inch, so slowly it's invisible, you manage to look over the top of the scope tube through the grass-fringed edge of the hole. Your gaze climbs the tree, checking each crotch, boring into every clump of leaves. But there's nothing there except the bait. The bait? Jesus.

Your hands are shaking as you get down to the scope again. As you peer through, your heart hammers and you feel strangled on your own breath. The view through the cross hairs shows nothing but a solid field of gold, black, and amber rosettes. How he got there, you'll never know. But he is definitely not an optical illusion. You haven't felt like this since your first football game, that first date in the back of the '49 Ford, or the sight of your first buck deer. You are a grown man now, but your hands shake like a hot crap shooter, and if one more drop of sweat slides into your eyes, you know you'll go stark blind. The pressure of the pro's hand is firm, pulsing slightly as you continue to stare in complete disbelief at what you're seeing.

A teensy move of the rifle fills the lens with the face of the big cat. Fascinated, you can't decide whether his eyes are yellow or green, but there is clearly a bloated tick on the side of his head under his ear. Great God, but with that gore-covered muzzle, he sure doesn't look like anything you ever saw in a zoo! You try to hold the rifle steady as the cross hairs slip to the right and down the neck, stopping to throb and bounce on the center of his shoulder. The corrugation of the trigger surface feels crisp on your fingertip as you start to squeeze, desperately praying that the gun will quit moving around. Just before the sear slips and the firing pin falls, the scope is magically empty. Somehow, he has moved.

Slowly, but with rising panic, you try to pick him up again, relief flooding back as a paw shows and the big post slides back up, now holding better on the middle of his chest. You remember what the pro told you and try to lock in onto a single rosette and blow the center out of it. The shot scares you. As the unfelt kick knocks you back, another blast of thunder chooses that instant to explode. Of course, you've lost him, but it dawns on you over all the noise that the professional is shouting something. As if through a haze, you realize that it's a warning. "Watch it! Goddammit! Watch it!" You are knocked aside and the roar of a shotgun slaps you with muzzle concussion. Then, as if a vault door has slammed, everything is silent.

The hunter is leaning over the top of the "hide," pointing down with the twin muzzles of the Greener. He is dead still as the seconds tick by, a sweaty, scruffy, acrid statue that blends with the powder smoke covering something half-hidden in the grass three yards to the front. At last, he half-relaxes and, the gun still ready, pushes through the shaggy front of the "hide" into the open. You follow him.

At first, even at this distance he's a perfect blend of broken outline. But for the growing rivulet of blood running out of the corner of his mouth and the shining greenish-yellow jade of his eyes, you wouldn't be able to see him yet. For sure, he is dead. "Sonovabitch," mutters the professional with a touch of gentle reverence. "Looked for a minute as if we were gonna have visitors."

"What happened?" you ask, realizing that sounds slightly dumb.

"You didn't see? Ah, lost him in the recoil." The hunter lights a pair of cigarettes and passes one to Silent, who is at the leopard's side, cautiously touching the unblinking eye with his spear point. Despite the glowing tip, he takes it flat in leathery hands. It doesn't seem to hurt. "Well," continues the pro, his speech visible in a series of blue smoke puffs, "you hit him just fine. Heart. Here, take a look." You follow his indication with the muzzle of the scatter-gun and see the tunnel blown by the .375 through the chest.

"I know he was dead. You know he was dead. He didn't. Fell out of that tree and about halfway to the ground, righted himself, and came for the 'hide' like a scalded greyhound. Probably thought we were a nice thick bunch of bush." He exhales again and takes a fresh drag. A fat drop of rain thumps the back of your hand. "Sorry I had to bust him, but things were a little crowded in here as it was. I don't think he even knew we were here."

Silent has driven in the pegs and is holding the steel tape by one end. "Uh, huh," says the hunter to himself. "Seven-one. Big chap. Congratulations."

You shake hands, not at all sorry for the fact that the buckshot has messed him up a bit. Consider the alternative. "Oh, the hell with it," you hear yourself say. "Give me a bloody cigarette." After three years, it tastes very good indeed.

6 LION

I ADJUSTED the squelch dial on the SSB radio, dust-dirty thumb on the transmit toggle of the microphone, listening to the hollow voice of the Chief Game Officer 150 miles down the valley. Bloody hell, but I hated that radio. In itself, that didn't make much sense, for it was my only link to the dream world where water runs through a pipe uncontaminated by snail flukes, where there are mattressed beds, marbled beefsteaks, and girls that smelled good and giggled. To be fair, it wasn't only the radio. Sometimes big trouble came by sweating runner, frightened boy, or just by being in the wrong place at the right time. But mostly it was that damn radio.

I never had it on any more than I could help, and in the dry season it just sat on a high stump under a small thatched cover to prevent the sun from melting it into slag. Red and black alligator-clamped leads snarled their way to my hunting car's battery when I had a "sched," and at least there was always a great laugh to be had when a newly assigned game guard was asked to "steady" the naked wire when I transmitted. When I pressed the my-turn button to broadcast, that antenna practically glowed, although I am sufficiently Man Primeval to have never bothered to ask why. I loathe two-way radios, taxes, and politics, approximately in that order. But when you're a Game Control Officer in Zambia's northern and eastern provinces, you realize that the SSB is just a fact of life. Or death. You listen up. Very carefully.

Taking a despairing toss of the plastic "glass" of lukewarm scotch, I stared at the beady, impersonal dial-eyes and dull casing of the unit as the voice droned on as if coming from the other end of a sewer.

". . . So it crossed the river into the reserve, and you'll just have to head down there and take care of it. Roger? Over."

I figured I'd better cover my woolgathering. "Ahhmm, sir, I had some, er, reception difficulties with the earlier portion of your message. Would you repeat the essentials, please? Over."

My thumb relaxed, and the toggle sprang back to receive. That's it. Be firm. Professional. I sensed an exasperated official sigh on the other end before the speaker crackled again.

"I *said* that Hanson, down at Imvubu Camp, has lost a wounded lion that crossed the river into the reserve. You know that nobody is permitted in there except Game Department personnel. You must go down to Imvubu, find out the details, and follow up the lion before he bumps into somebody or turns man-eater. Do you understand? Over." Click.

Oh, brother, did I ever understand. The safari concession area, leased by the government to a private outfitting firm, bordered the Northern Luangwa Game Reserve, separated only by the Luangwa River. Along

194

the hundred-odd miles that the concession stretched were seven or eight camps conducting safaris. In fact, one of them had once been mine before I joined the Game Department in a moment of impetuous idiocy that I believed would spawn a Great African Novel. I could go back to the States and have a Park Avenue penthouse and a Spanish castle like Bob Ruark, or maybe take a crack at Papa's daiquiri record between depositing all those filthy, capitalistic royalties. Instead, I had cornered the local market on ringworm and indigestion. Over the past couple of seasons, things were bleak except for a couple of rip-roaring leaves to Lusaka, and I had been forced to the conclusion that I was not on Kismet's preferred list. Lots of things tried to bite me. My hair didn't silver majestically at the temples like Stewart Granger's, it just sort of fell out in clumps from time to time. Still, it beat the 7:17 A.M. from Mountain Station to the Hoboken Tubes all hollow. This was a tough and sometimes hairy existence, but that life was *really* scary.

Well, back to the Heroic Deeds Department. That's me, Boy Paladin. Maidens Rescued, Dragons Slain, Philistines Smitten. We also deal in other people's wounded lions, by appointment only. Major Credit Cards. Get a grip on yourself, boy. Press the talk button and tell the nice man you understand. But don't tell him what you think of the idea. You might get sent back to Wall Street for thirty-to-life.

"Roger, chief, I've got it. I'll leave in the morning. Roger that? Over."

"Officer Capstick. [Look out, here it comes.] I have *told* you not to call me 'chief.' Further, that is not a roger. You will leave tonight. As you Yanks say, 'as in now.' Acknowledge. Over."

"Affirmative, ch—. . . uh, sir. Packing my *katundu*

195

now. Will contact you upon my return. Over and out."

"Headquarters out." Click. Hisssss.

It was almost midnight under a drifting, tarnished coin of moon when I saw the first pressure lamps of George Hanson's camp flashing like an insane Morse code through the gnarled hardwoods along the river. I parked the 'Rover next to his Toyota Land Cruiser and saw George walking toward me from the campfire with one of his men, who hustled my rifle and light baggage off to a client hut. My gunbearer Silent disappeared into the silver-tinged darkness toward the gunbearers' hut, his sleeping mat and blanket over his shoulder. I shook hands with George and shot him a zinger. We were old friends, having done several four-client safaris together in the past, and I knew how embarrassed he would be over having lost a lion.

Over a nightcap with his client, a lawyer from Chicago, George told me what had happened. They had stalked a bait they had hung after cutting some impressive tracks. Sure enough, at first light they spotted the lion and two lionesses sauntering away for a drink and a snooze after feeding. The client fired but clipped the male a bit too far back. It reared in the air, biting at its flank, then streaked off into heavy cover before George could stick in a finisher.

George topped up our snifters and stirred the blue licks of *mopane* wood fire into hungry tongues of red. Below us, the honking of a pair of hippos echoed hollowly up the watercourse.

"I went in after him, Pedro," said the big Rhodesian thoughtfully. "But he'd gotten a better offer. Nobody home. So I went on through the thick stuff to the river bank, and sure as rain, there was our boy just climbing out on the other side. An easy shot." He paused, lit a cigarette from the fire, and glanced sideways at me. "But, then, we both know the rules, don't we?"

It was crazy, but George was right. If he'd taken the shot and anchored the lion, he would have been indisputably guilty of lion poaching, as the cat was standing in the game reserve once he'd reached the far bank. No ifs, ands, or buts. He surely would have been turned in by one of the camp informers for a reward, lost his professional ticket, and perhaps been the guest of Zambian civil authorities in some very substandard housing for six months or so. He was mighty smart not to have taken the shot, no matter how much trouble it would have saved me. Following procedure, he had raised the "chief," and it was now my problem. He couldn't even come with me into the reserve to follow up the wounded lion, although I knew it galled him. I assure you, America's claim to overlegislation is not exclusive.

Tomorrow, Silent (who technically would also be a trespasser) and I would have a look-see. Meanwhile, I stretched my carcass out between the crisp white sheets of a real bed in the spare client hut, wondering vaguely if they'd be pulling those same sheets over my face tomorrow. If you haven't heard, wounded lions are singularly unpleasant creatures, definitely inclined toward the subdivision of follow-up hunters into small, bloody chunks, which can absolutely ruin your vacation. Hoping that the bullet may have, after all, proved fatal and that the cat was lying dead on the other bank, I slipped my brain into neutral and dozed off.

I awoke on the verge of a breakthrough, possibly a refinement of the space-time continuum: Dawn comes faster in direct proportion to the number of brandies one drinks the night before. The blackness had evaporated in about half the time it normally takes. One of Hanson's waiters politely placed a mug of sweet, strong, milky tea on the cane top of the small table next to the bed. I swilled it, treated myself to a shower and a shave, and walked over to the dining hut with its lovely river view. George was already at breakfast with his client. Pointing over a plate of eggs and—wonder of wonders—bacon, he indicated the place where the lion had crossed, about two miles straight upriver near a slow bend. Knowing the area well from previous safaris, I mentally marked a small, shallow ford within a few hundred yards of the lion's crossing and helped myself to seconds.

Checking out the .470 Nitro Evans double rifle and switching to soft-point ammo from my customary solids, I had Silent fill a flax jawsack with filtered water and filched some biltong from George for lunch.

With Hanson leading the way, we returned to the site of the wounding for a look around. Hanson figured that the bullet had been far enough back to cause intestinal damage, and as he is a fine pro, I took his word for it. The lion had been hit with a .458 Winchester Magnum, a 510-grain soft-point, which I knew from experience meant that there would be no exit hole on the far side. I've seen fifteen or more lions shot broadside with that bullet, and while it looks mighty good on the ballistics charts, it just won't shoot completely through a lion. The problem with the squat bullet may be that of overexpansion, preventing the excess penetration so desirable. This is a great disadvantage of the load; two holes instead of one make tracking a helluva lot easier and also bring on blood-loss shock much more quickly. Sure, you can kill lions with 510-grain, .458 Mag soft-points, but it's not the size of the hole that matters. It's where it's located.

I asked George about our wounded swain's lady friends, and he told me that they had, in the confusion of the moment, just disappeared and were not seen crossing the river with the old man. Of course, that didn't mean that they hadn't crossed later. But just maybe, for once, luck was swinging my way, and we could concentrate on the male without worrying about the girls. Back in East Africa, when lions were considered vermin, the old-timers usually shot the female first, as she was the more likely to charge under most circumstances. And I can promise you that they were right, not that the male is in the least inhibited when wounded or angry or perhaps simply in the mood for a human-type turkey on rye. Like me.

I sent Silent, carrying his throwing spear (the same one, incidentally, with which I had managed to kill the Chabunkwa man-eating lion, while Silent fed him an arm so that I could recover from a terrific wallop taken in a point-blank charge) to check the spoor in the softer dirt and sand at the water's edge. This way he would know and recognize the tracks when we took up the trail on the far bank. I have always, with indeterminate validity, reckoned myself a good tracker, but one glance at a set of tracks left an indelible impression on Silent's memory as effective as an enlarged color photograph. He was not officially a member of the Game Department, so I paid him from my own meager wages. We had hunted together for so long that we hardly ever even spoke in the bush, each somehow blending his mind with the other. You don't walk away from a relationship like that; ask anybody who's spent time under fire with trusted companions.

"*Yena kona mukulu stelik, Bwana,*" he said, which meant that the lion was something of a large fellow. He wrinkled his forehead thoughtfully and lit a ferocious creation of black shag tobacco wrapped in newspaper.

"*Wena zo azi lo mkondo?*" I asked him teasingly. "Will you remember the spoor?"

He chuckled low, dragging on the half-cigarette, half-bushfire. "Like that of my youngest wife, Bwana," he answered in Fanagalo. "Now let us go like men and make an end to this play of children."

This one-upmanship was for the benefit of George's hunting staff, who were minutely examining the sky and the tops of their bare, dusty feet. There is always a great rivalry among Africans who serve a hunter, even to the extent that, if a really big elephant is killed and the walk back to the vehicle is twenty miles or more, they will almost come to blows deciding who will have the prestige of carrying the heaviest tusk, despite the great extra effort required. Pride makes a good safari crew, and Silent was regarded as almost a legend among other gunbearers.

Well, I thought, starting for the ford, might as well get going, can't dance anyway. With desert boots hung around my neck by the laces, I crossed first, the big double ready, keeping a sharp eye for crocs in this infested water. It was only knee-deep here in the dry season, and we headed straight up the bank to the point opposite the tracks on the other side. There they were, still crisp, about twenty-four hours old, which tallied with the timing of the wounding. And Silent was right. The pug marks were deep and broad—a very large pussycat. I tried to picture him somewhere ahead, knowing that his mane was full and quite reddish, a fact I had discovered from George so I didn't happen into another big male and bust him by mistake. We started directly on the trail, an error I will not likely repeat.

Real dried blood began to show about 150 yards into the heavy riverine bush, the cat having dried off enough that the oozings were no longer diluted by the water dripping off his hide. The greenest beginner could tell that it was a gut wound and not bleeding heavily, as the bullet entrance hole was alternately covered and uncovered by the sliding action of the cat's skin as he walked. Not good. With the pain, he'd be savage as a boxcar full of honey badgers, but the big, fat slug had done structural damage that would slow him down. Okay now, take it cool. Just because the track looks cold doesn't mean that he isn't under the next shady bush, licking his wounds, waiting for you. I sidestepped and immediately Silent passed me, hunched over, his eyes locked like a laser on the almost invisible spoor as I scanned ahead and to the sides, trying to make visual contact before a surprise charge. There are probably more dangerous aspects to the world of big game hunting, but the following up of gut-shot lions has got to rank high simply because so many good hunters have gotten the Big Chop doing it.

I'd done it enough to know what to expect: the low, blinding rush; the hard grunts and lash of tail; the blur of white fangs; the shock of realizing that *it was coming* and you had a second, maybe less, to place a perfect shot into the vitals of the streaking target. Goalies can let the puck or soccer ball slip past them and suffer no more than chagrin. The best pass receiver in professional football can drop a floater wide open in the end zone of the Super Bowl and, at worst, he'll lose the game and a few nights of sleep. But you can't *ever* drop a pass with a wounded lion. No mistakes without paying the price. And that gets extremely expensive—you don't get embarrassed, you get dead.

After two hours, we had covered about six hundred

yards inland from the river. Twice the cat had stopped and bedded down, only to rise and continue again. At the last spot, in the shady lee of an elephant-damaged sausage tree, there was a fair patch of blood not much more than an hour old. Silent rubbed it between his fingers and rolled his malarial eyes up at me. I jerked my chin forward and looked over the rifle, making sure the sights were clear. I gripped two extra rounds between left-hand fingers.

I was puzzled that the lion had moved so far from the heavier bush and the convenience of water, although there was still enough low bush and grass to hide a full-blown menagerie in ten square yards. It was getting hot now, and I don't just mean the sun. I could sense the presence of the lion almost the way one can feel a stare from across a cocktail party on the back of the neck. He was there, all right, and bloody close.

The warning snarl was as flat and sharp as a butcher's cleaver. It came from a clump of grassy bush thirty yards in front of us. Instantly, Silent cleared my field of fire in a single, sinuous movement. He moved to my side, erect, his spear poised. I watched the spot over the wide vee of express sights as another menacing mumble joined the first growl. Uh-oh. Not in the script. I could see tawny but indistinct movement as the lions, however many there were, flattened themselves, the volume of their threats growing. Better grab the initiative, I thought, before they take it away from you, and formed the soundless word *litye* to Silent. He glanced down, looking for something to throw. Of course, I had forgotten that there are no stones in the Luangwa Valley, but he caught my meaning and pulled out several extra rounds he was carrying for the .470 and began to lob them into the thicket. *That did it!*

The first thing I saw was the shaggy auburn head of the big male as he cleared the thicket, starting his charge. I just lowered the sights a hair and touched off at his chest, collapsing him as if he'd been hit by a thunderbolt. In the same half-second, two lionesses popped out in a semicharge and stopped, undecided, fifteen yards short. They crouched flat, their tails lashing, practically blowing off my bush shorts with their growling. They were most upset, but they didn't charge—at least not yet they didn't. African standoff. But it was now their move. And they were holding all the spades.

Interesting situation, especially if you are there. Two very angry lionesses within leaping range and one cartridge left in the rifle. Yes, you may shoot one, but even with the years of experience, there's no way to break the rifle and reload before the other one nails you. Just too close. Maybe Silent can stick the survivor and give you enough time, but that's mighty dicey and will likely lead to a hell of a lot of stitches for somebody. There's also the red tape reports in quintuplicate as well as the inquiry if you pound anything, even in self-defense, in the reserve. Will they both charge? That's easy. They will unless they don't. Odds say yes, and together. As your brain races, one slithers another yard closer, and you can't help but marvel at the smooth flow of incredible muscles under the rippling skin. But you'd better make up your mind right quick, 'cause they look like they're gonna come.

Carefully, so slowly as to be hardly noticeable, you and Silent begin to back off. That's it. Nice and easy. See, girls? Nothing to get upset about. The growling intensifies but nothing happens. Another yard. Two more. They're bluffing, you hope. Finally, you think you have enough room to manage loading a fresh round, particularly if you can gain a large chunk of a second to confuse them. You glance at Silent again and he nods, just a twitch of the head. "Eeeee-yaaaahhh!" you scream and boom the second barrel into the ground right between them, the bullet throwing stinging sand and dirt as you flip the locking lever to open the breech. The empties ping clear, and with almost simultaneous metallic "tonks," fresh rounds slip home. The breech of the Evans closes with the finality and precision of a bank vault.

Oh-kaayy. Now it's your turn again. If you can't take two lionesses even in a double charge over twenty-five fairly open yards, especially with one already dead in the sights, you deserve whatever you get. Shouting, you start to move back toward them: one has done a back flip at the shot and wears an expression that plainly says that maybe this wasn't such a good idea after all. As if on signal, first one, then the other give final, sneering snarls and dash off to the side. You and Silent look at each other. *Yebo.* It was a *close* thing.

The male is lying dead in full stride, his mouth full of blood and sandy dirt. The 500-grain Kynoch has caught him right under the chin, just as he began his first low bound. But your private rules are never broken, and you give him another dose just to be supersure. You pick up the cartridges Silent had thrown and start to piece the whole thing together.

It took about a mile of walking to sort out the spoor once we had camouflaged the body of the lion to keep the vultures off. He had come so far from the river because the females, unbeknownst to George or us, had also crossed during the night, but farther upstream. They had missed the male's spoor and had probably called to him, which drew him out of the

204

really thick cover and away from the water. The tracks
of the two lionesses were finally located on the river
bank a thousand yards upstream from the point where
the male crossed. Had we really done our homework,
we would have known what we had to deal with. Oh,
well, live and learn. It sure beats the alternative.

A good case could probably be made for designating
lion hunting the oldest dangerous sport in the world.
The caves of Europe, where the lion was very much a
part of the somewhat toothy landscape, were painted
and engraved with images of lions by early Neolithic
hunters. The Middle East, where lions were not only
numerous but a major health hazard, is also rich with
references to huge hunts starring the monarch of the
moment, who normally hunted from his chariot with
bow or javelin. Records from the Middle East date
from thousands of years before Christ. Some of the
reliefs from Nineveh are particularly spectacular, dat-
ing from the reign of Ashurbanipal II (sixth century
B.C.) and showing detailed scenes of the king hunting
lions. One series from Kalacha features the ruler in his
chariot wheeling past a dying male with two arrows in
him. Another is famous for its elegant artwork depic-
tion of Ashurbanipal trying to keep off a lion with his
lance and later on foot trying to place a killing arrow
into a wounded cat while his shield bearer protects the
royal hindside and offers a spear in case of a charge.
There are lions all over the place; one with an arrow
in his neck tries to eat the king's chariot wheel while
another, a lioness crippled by a shaft in the spine,
drags herself forward with a still-scary snarl.
   That the lion was one of the favorite subjects of almost any medium of art is a pretty good indication of
the awe in which he was and is held. Even today, he is

found everywhere from the steps of public libraries to postage stamps, from bronzes to statues, from flags to beer brands. My own family's heraldic device contains a lion *rampant,* and a painting of a pair of lions is the central feature of the living room at home. Ah, but there's nothing like the real thing. . . .

After the tiger, the African lion is the biggest feline carnivore on earth, surpassed in the category of land animals only by the bear. As is the case with many impressive predators, the size of a healthy adult is usually overestimated, and a lion that tips four hundred pounds live weight is a mighty big one indeed. However, if you've never seen a lion's carcass after the hide is removed, you probably don't appreciate that there is virtually no spare baggage aboard. The musculature of a lion is perfectly astonishing and lends credence to the great feats of strength attributed to the species over the years. A particularly large lion will stand around thirty-eight to forty-two inches at the shoulder and have a between-the-pegs length (determined by driving vertical stakes into the ground at the nose and at the tip of the tail of the dead animal and taping between the pegs rather than following the longer body contours) of around nine feet. There are much bigger ones on record, including a tabbie, killed in Angola in 1973, that was confirmed by *Rowland Ward's* as eleven feet even. Lord Wolverton, who hunted in Somalia in the 1890s (amusing himself and his two companions, accompanied by some eighty soldiers, by capturing and putting a large bandit tribe to the lash as well as burning its village), was credited by C. A. W. Guggisberg, who wrote *Simba,* the handbook on lions, as having taken one lion measuring ten feet ten inches. I believe that Guggisberg was misled by Lord Wolverton's reference to the lion's length, for in *Sport in Somaliland,* Wolverton says that the lion was the reported length "when pegged out." There is a big difference between length determined after "pegging out" the skin, which is removed from the animal and staked to the ground to be cured with salt and alum, and length determined *"between* the pegs," which is done before skinning. Still, it must have been a mighty big lion.

One lion is imposing enough, but when it comes to numbers, I find myself recalling a late afternoon in Ngamiland, in northwestern Botswana, back in the early 1970s. I was in a leopard blind, watching the flies crawl in and out of the spearholes in a warthog—my tracker, Debalo, speared it to help it decay faster— serving as bait in a tree forty yards off. The greater the—to put it delicately—scent, the sooner a leopard would find it, and one had. With me, scrunched on camp stools, was a couple from Iowa, Debalo covering the rear of the flimsy blind with his spear against housebreakers. The sun was setting like a clip from a tourist board commercial over the Okavango Swamps, and I had a feeling that we would get a shot in the next few minutes.

Lighting a smoke from the butt of the last cigarette so as not to make a noise by scraping a match, I stared through the little binoculars at the grass surrounding the base of the tree and felt my hackles start to squirm like nightwalkers doing the India rope trick. From a hundred yards off, invisible through the murky late bush shadows, came a thud of hooves and a rasping mutter that could only mean lions. Faster than you could think, a zebra mare burst into sight, running flat-out with a pair of tawny shapes behind and alongside her. Not twenty yards from the front of the blind, directly between us and the bait tree, an old lioness lunged, half-boarded the zebra, and brought her down in a depth charge of flying dirt. With my mouth hanging open like a flytrap, I saw her grab the zebra by the throat, shifting her bite from the back of the neck as she brought the kicking, squealing mare into a thrashing heap. For a full minute she hung on, crushing the windpipe until the last quiver quit. The younger lioness accompanying the killer began to bite at the stomach and was growled off just as the bush parted and three more lions raced up. There was a single quarter-grown cub, a magnificent male, and another lioness.

We watched for a couple seconds through vision slits in the blind—dumbfounded, speaking for myself—as the passel of lions swarmed over their meal. Lord Almighty, but what were the odds of a hunting pride of lions picking the one place in scads of square miles that would put them within rock-throwing range of a delicate, sensitive, easily upset chap like myself? My client and his wife were shocked stiff enough that you could have put price tags on them had you been looking for some rather *avant-garde* statuary. It may sound interesting now, but it sure as hell wasn't funny that September dusk.

It was starting to get dark. Real, African *dark* dark. The sun was half-past the hairy horizon and I knew that once it was gone, things would definitely not become boring. With a major banquet in progress sixty feet away, so close that every crunch of gristle and slobber of wet red meat came through the grass walls of the blind like gourmet night at the Bronx Zoo, I knew we had to do something pretty quick. We, as in me.

208

I considered our firepower: one spear clutched in ivory knuckles by a Bushman with such good sense he's too scared to turn around, a .300 Winchester Magnum strangled between the even whiter fingers of an American businessman who is starting to wish he'd gone bankrupt rather than be able to afford this safari, a thoroughly scared American lady who looks as if she's going to shriek the bark off the nearby trees if she can ever catch her breath, and a Model 12 Winchester 12-gauge pump shotgun with the magazine plug removed, offering seven Magnum loads of buckshot. Never mind the color of my knuckles. I've always had pale knuckles. It's from my mother's side of the family.

The problem is proximity, and I have a hunch the lions will not construe it as their fault. We are so close that it's almost impossible to crawl away without being heard or spotted, and Botswana lions, who are not known for commenting that they just love people, except in a culinary sense, may feel obliged to drop by for a quick bite. The big male is the sort that must have haunted L. B. Mayer's happier dreams, a ridiculously thick neck toupee supported by something near ten feet of *Tau,* which is the polite name for lions in Ngamiland where, among other things, Tswana is spoken. I don't think it will do to drape Debalo's loincloth over my arm, march up, and introduce myself as their waiter. Debalo's very sensitive, anyway. In any case, it's getting even darker even more quickly. The Land Rover is still five hundred yards away, featuring a dozing Simone, my gunbearer, at the wheel.

As the sun leaves only a smoothly milled edge over the swamps, I consider the timing. Timing has not

been my high point on this safari, or we would cool
the big boy with the greatest of ease at this range and I
would happily take the consequences of backing off
from his ladies fair. Alas, on the fifth day out, we had
found a pair of *Tau* in the heat of midday, loafing in
the shade of a big thorn clump, and my client made a
perfect heart shot.

On the wrong one.

Oh, it was a passable tomcat, pushing nine feet and
with slightly more hair than I have, which isn't saying
all that much. The male I had indicated looked like
the "after" part of a scalp rehabilitation advertisement
in a pulp magazine, but the client never saw him until
he had busted the little brother. Oh, well, *sic transit*
large gratuities. One lion per customer. That was his.
If I have to give some large-caliber persuasion to the
gang here assembled, it will mean legal difficulties
which will involve my proving my innocence rather
than the more traditional legal approach to the felony.
Weird things flit through your brain, the old Jell-O ad,
for instance: busy day, busy day, no time to make dessert. What you want not to do is provide it.

Well, I'm theoretically an American. What about
the cavalry? Simone has been told to come if he hears
a shot before dark, which was hopefully to have been
the signal of the leopard's demise. If there's no shot,
he will come at dark, when the legal right to shoot
expires. Should I wait for dark? What will happen if I
fire now to signal him? Will he be swarmed by legions
of lions or will they decide they forgot to leave a tip at
their last meal? With a touch of light, I believe I can
hold the fort until the car pitches up, but after dark,
all the odds go over to the lions.

I have a torch—a five-celled Kel-Lite flashlight of
blued steel that lies next to the typewriter as I clack

this out. Its serial number is 116885 and it bears, among other scars of honor, a large dent in the shaft where I expanded the horizons of a poacher who tried to practice a bit of surgery on me in Zambia. It has also a few exploratory bites from the jaws of at least one hyena who took a curious interest in the wads of dried mealie meal or corn porridge forever mummified into the checkering by my various staff after eating before washing their hands off.

You can see your hand in front of your face if you're so inclined, but not much more. I press the two clients to the back of the blind and sign to Debalo that he will be the bait the next time we have a request for hyenas if he doesn't cover them. Digging a couple of extra shells out of my pocket, I hold them in my left hand, flip on the flagrant, probing beam of the torch and fire the shotgun over the lions. They are not pleased. With the Winchester barrel insulated from the light by a couple of fingers so the recoil won't break the bulb's filament, I risk a sweeping wash of light. The dead zebra stands out like a new pinstripe suit, as do a large number of eyes, dazzled but advancing. I work the pump and let off another round. To my extreme delight, they stop, considering, I presume, the quality of my obviously stringy cutlets. A roar from one of the cats hits us across the face as solidly as a blow.

Fumbling, I stuff two replacement rounds into the gorge of the Model 12, which digests them with a slithering sound and thankfully without mechanical gagging. Behind us, I can hear the whine of the hunting car, laboring under the indelicate hand and foot of Simone who does not, possibly on religious grounds, believe in such things as second gear. If the *motorgharri* goes, it goes. What matter the sound?

Speaking aloud between shouts I hope sound intimidating, I push the whole reluctant group out the back of the blind. Across the bush-stubbled plain, Simone's headlights goose the dark like twin fingers, while he labors happily along in first. I squirt the lion pride with another dose of flashlight. Only three pairs of eyes flash back green-gold. Hey, where's everybody gone? Swinging to the side, I pick up a grassy-dun form. A lioness flanking. Bugger this lot! I shoot her in the tail, aiming as carefully as possible to avoid crippling her. She blows leaves off the trees in pain, flips over, and runs off at a tangent. "*Buya,* godbloodydammit," I screech at the dawdling Simone, pictures of the Christian martyrs coloring my thoughts. He of course has no idea what's going on. The lady is hysterical, complete with sobbing, praying, and even some rather original and astonishingly colorful cursing. The client still looks as if somebody stuck toothpicks between his eyelids vertically. Happily, I'm writing this and will not record what I may have looked like. The privilege of the profession.

Simone finally arrives, we all bundle in the open car, and I take over the driver's seat by essentially levering Simone bodily over the front seat. People may call me a lot of things, but "little" isn't one I hear very often. I popped the clutch, fired the scatter-gun again, and we made tracks, the casts of which would be no mean addition to any museum's collection of Africana, until we were back to camp.

There's nothing funny about being truly, genuinely frightened, as my clients showed by the lady's literally collapsing from nervous tension and my gentleman's doing unspeakable things to a bottle and more of Haig Pinch. We hunted ducks and sand grouse the next day, for which I may have been the most grateful. Incidentally, we did get the leopard, better than two inches into the book, five evenings later. I looked for that male lion for the following two months with new clients, but, as might be expected, nobody ever shows up when you want them to.

I hadn't liked actually shooting the lioness in the tail, but she had acted pretty blasé about the swarms of buckshot I had been spreading above the group. Anyway, she was far enough off that the pattern would have only put one or two pellets into her rudder at most, painful but hardly enough to require following her up. Obviously, I never thought to mention it to the Game Department. . . .

Kenya in the old days was a grand place for the sport adopted by the British and Afrikaaner settlers known as "galloping" lions. Of course, it was dangerous as typhoid, but then the men who dragged the infant Kenya colony out of the virgin bush into the twentieth century were not exactly shy, either. The elements required for an afternoon of this monotony-breaking pastime were a fast horse, a good rifle, a few lions on an open plain, and not much concern for the future. When Teddy Roosevelt was there on safari near the still-shantytown of Nairobi in 1909, he spent time with many of the great lion hunters of the region and also learned why a few others weren't around. Sir George Grey was killed by a lion on the Athi Plains when his light .280 Ross bullet failed to anchor a big male, which bit him to death. Grey's brother, Sir Edward, the British foreign minister, was later killed by a wounded Cape buffalo. It must have run in the family.

Teddy Roosevelt also recounted the misadventure of two stalwarts named Lucas and Goldfinch, a settler and a game warden, respectively. Not too far from the spot where an English officer called Stewart took on his first and last lion—the lion won—these two followed a lion they had chased into a bit of bush, bringing their horses too close in their eagerness. Even then it was considered axiomatic that the horse was never foaled that from a standing start could escape a lion at a distance of twenty-five yards or fewer, an unfortunate fact of animal physiology that Lucas and Goldfinch turned into an immutable law. The lion flipped on his afterburner and rocketed out, shredding Goldfinch before he could get his mount out of the way. Lucas turned his horse in an attempt to help as he saw the lion savaging his friend. The lion left the nearly dead Goldfinch and flattened Lucas, pinning him down under teeth and claws. Despite heavy loss of blood, Goldfinch crawled over to his rifle, took aim, and killed the lion before collapsing himself. He remained crippled for life. The gallant Lucas died. Helluva lot of fun, chaps, lion hunting on horseback.

There were better-known sportsmen in Kenya in those days than the locals who merely hunted lion as a matter of course; including Sir Alfred Pease, Lord Delamere, Blayney Percival, Governor Jackson, Frederick Selous, and the Hill cousins, Harold and Clifford. The list is huge and its members still well remembered, not only for their daring but also for their injuries and their deaths.

Among wholesale lots of well-known European sportsmen who were killed in the 1920s were the Hungarian Count Hunyady, who perished in the Sudan in 1923, and Bernard de Watteville, a Swiss. Both died of gangrene resulting from infected lion wounds. De Watteville was charged by the nineteenth lion he tried to kill on safari with his daughter, Vivienne. The Swiss was knocked flat the first time but was not hurt. The lion didn't make the same mistake twice, badly mauling him in a second charge. De Watteville was somehow able to stick his rifle's muzzle into the lion's neck and kill it. Unfortunately, he was so tangled up with the gang hooks of the lion's claws that he finally had to rip them out of his own meat one at a time. Refusing aid, he then forced himself into the 2-hour walk back to camp, where Vivienne was ill with malaria. It must have been quite a feat even to get there, for upon arrival the bandaging alone took three hours. His right arm and hand were shredded, as were both legs. In the two hours before he was disinfected, the deadly septicemia that is produced by the layer of rotting meat under the lions' claws and on their teeth and that leads to blood poisoning and gangrene, had had more than enough time to work. As the sun set the next day, the man was dead.

Dr. Emile Gromier, famous medico and naturalist in what was then French Equatorial Africa, wrote of the awful condition of a Game Officer he treated nine days after the man, Bruneau de Laborie, had been mauled in the arm by a lion. "The hand and forearm were only a greenish mass," wrote Gromier, "the bones were splintered and gangrene had already reached the shoulder." A complication developed under the process of amputation, ringing up but one more score for *Simba.*

The father of Lloyd Wilmot, whom I knew slightly in Botswana and who ran Crocodile Camp Lodge near Maun, survived a terrific going-over from a lion while a Tsetse Control Officer for what was then the Bechuanaland government. Cronje Wilmot, who weathered the lion attack only to be later killed by what was believed to be a black mamba, got caught by a wounded lion that nailed him from a piece of cover.

The first bite drove the canines all the way through the left calf, shattering the shin bones in the process. As the fight went on, Wilmot caught another dose in the hip, and when he tried to protect his head, was severely bitten in the hand. For some reason, the lion then ran off a few yards, giving Wilmot the chance to recover his rifle and pot the blighter. The Fly Officer had twenty-three bite holes as well as some scratches but survived in fair shape. Survival after a grappling with a 400-pound wounded lion in itself is pretty noteworthy.

Simba often shows unsure table manners about just what to do with a human when he catches up with one that has bestirred his ire. Lion charges are among the great classic animal behavior patterns of Africa that you definitely do not want to become overfamiliar with, but they're still worth a discussion here.

Like most big game, the lion will bluff-charge in an attempt to shoo off anything that's disturbing it. As with the rest of the Big Five, it's very difficult to tell what's real and what isn't, and to find out can cost you your life with no credit for good behavior. I have been told that leopards will bluff but have never been so informed by anybody who I knew to have any real knowledge of the animal and his lightning-deadly habits. Maybe some of the preservationists wandering around African game parks, standing up to irritated lions through lack of saner options, will claim that they're nothing but big pussycats, but not this boy! And, at that, we're talking about unwounded lions, not those toting a first-degree grudge against somebody who put a painful hole in them.

Far and away the great preponderance of charging lions are those that have been wounded or at least molested. A lion with several hundred grains of East Alton, Illinois, cupro-jacketed irritation in his guts is certainly in the uncontested running for the title of Scariest Animal on Earth, and the preview of his proposed performance does little to deny this. A wounded lion will, like most other dangerous game, take to the nearest and most dense cover he can find. He'll usually advertise that he's coming with at least one or two grunts, maybe even full-blown vocal volcanics. Still, if you see him, the biggest clue is the tail. Of course, if you can see him, it's presumed that you should be able to dissuade him from his charge by blowing him out of the water before he gets going, but somehow it doesn't always work out that way. One major exception would be when there is more than one lion involved. The tail will twitch, perhaps once, maybe as many as four times. If and when it goes rigid, normally straight up as a cast-iron pipe, you'd better pack your bags, boy, 'cause you is about to have visitors. I very much believe that the lion uses his tail for balance in a charge just as a cheetah uses his as a counterweight when persuading a gazelle to stay for dinner. Whatever, it's an almost infallible sign. Should you have any questions on this point, stay away from tailless lions.

A lion starts off at the speed that most other Big Fivers can't manage even after they build up momentum. The leopard is smaller and faster, but I still think that whoever came up with the platitude "cat-quick" was thinking of old *Simba.* When he comes for you, there's no doubt about it. Considerably faster than a horse from a standing start, he barrels through the bush and grass, grunting in determination fit to give a crusader loose bowels. You'll read about his springing and otherwise wasting time and motion, but it's generally not so. The lion comes in a yellow-beige streak, low to the ground, in a gliding rush led by a vertical corona of mane bristling as if with static, a setting that surrounds a pearl and coral matrix of mouth the size of a reasonable watermelon.

How fast? Trust me, though I never timed one. I would guess around forty miles per hour; some say more, some less. Whatever, it is a very large package of claws, teeth, and determination that takes an astonishingly short time to get to you if you don't donate something over .375 caliber into it in one big hurry.

I have only—to date—had one lion catch up with me, and that instance I have related in my first book. It was a very short charge that culminated in the man-eater's actually slamming into me from the side, turning that quadrant of my body into a charcoal gray hue but somehow not biting me, although it demonstrated its marvelous dentition on Silent's arm. Mauling of the legs is the most common injury besides death, followed by the pulping of whatever accessories are in reach, such as arms and head. Of course, the reason one hears more about this sort of wound is that it isn't instantly fatal and victims get a chance to tell about the experience. I personally know at least a dozen people who have lived through lion maulings of the less determined type but have no familiarity at all with any human bitten in the body or thorax who has had the chance to write home about it.

The tendency of the lion to stay low when charging a man has probably saved more lives than anything else. A lot more is heard about old *Tau* or *Silwane* "springing" on people than is gospel, at least as far as my experience shows. A lion would have to raise itself to pull down a buffalo or a zebra, but whatever the reason, it almost never finishes a charge against a man with an elevating leap.

One man who almost surely owed his life to this fact was Kalman Kittenberger, a Hungarian hunter and naturalist who was primarily collecting birds for the Budapest Museum. In the area of what was presumably Mt. Kilimanjaro, given that his assistant was a WaChaga, a tribe that lives only in that area, Kittenberger wounded a maneless male lion in heavy grass with a muffed neck shot on June 11, 1904. Curiously, the rifle Kittenberger used was bought from the early German sportsman and wildlife photographer, C. G. Schillings, a 7-mm Mauser magazine model.

The lion was only forty yards off when the Hungarian fired, trying for the neck to preserve the skull as a museum specimen. Actually, part of Kittenberger ended up in the museum along with the lion's skin and bones!

At the shot, the lion collapsed and disappeared in the dense grass, and Kittenberger presumed it to be dead. The hunter called for the young Chaga to bring the camera and some help from the other two men he had back at camp, and the kid hightailed it off to do as he was told. The Hungarian, curious to see his prize, started wading through the long grass to the place where *Simba* had presumably expired. Ah, well, fools, drunks, and lion hunters . . .

An immensely impressive demonstration of vocal displeasure blew out of the grass, which shocked Kittenberger into raising his Mauser. Almost instantly, he was presented with an impending lion from near point-blank range. Keeping his nerve, the scientist lined up the sights and squeezed off a round straight for the center of the cat's skull. Or at least he tried to. There was the deadest sound in the world of hunting, the hollow thwack of a misfire, which must have seemed loud in its finality even over the snarls of the charging lion. Possibly Kittenberger had a chance to think something less than flattering about Schillings, who had sold him the rifle, before the lion slammed into his hip.

Decked from the impact, the Hungarian lay on his back, trying to feed the Mauser into the lion's business end. With the speed born of panic, he somehow jacked a fresh round into the chamber and stuck a bullet through the lion's eye which, if it did not enhance the lion's stature as a specimen, sure helped Kittenberger's tenure as a curator.

It all happened so quickly that the hunter was never certain how he acquired the sliced artery in his right wrist—which he tourniqueted with a handkerchief— nor exactly how he had become completely covered in blood. For sure, it wasn't all the lion's. As he hobbled along using the rifle as a crutch and leaving a big, broad, bright red highway of blood as his spoor, he realized that he was probably more badly hurt than he felt but was spared further contemplation of the problem by passing out cold. When he recovered from his blackout, he was relieved to find his men staring at him from over a bush. They were, however, so frightened by his butcher-shop appearance that they were about to take off until he bullied them into carrying him back to camp.

Kittenberger not only lived, he showed a shade of what used to be called "colorful behavior" when I was back at the University of Virginia. Since the safari was just about at an end, he had foolishly traded most of his medical supplies for food and what he called "objects of ethnographical value." Perhaps a couple of slave girls? Okay, that was unworthy. In any case, he bound himself up with some strips of the cotton cloth he had on hand and almost as an afterthought amputated his badly injured right middle finger. I know you would have liked Kittenberger, for he then put the cut-off finger into a bottle of alcohol and shipped it off to the Budapest Museum with the rest of his specimens. It certainly arrived there and was taken seriously because, as the man later learned, the museum staff had noticed the clear signs of arsenic poisoning under the fingernail of the grisly trophy and commented on how dedicated he had obviously been in his collecting of birds. In those days, arsenic was used as a primary agent to preserve bird skins.

Kittenberger had a most uncomfortable time of getting himself evacuated, his wounds having turned horribly painful as he was being carried to help. Suffering terribly from thirst because his men had been run off a water hole by a group of unsociable elephants on the Rau River, he finally arrived at the settlement of Moshi only to find that the doctor there had himself been removed because of liver ulcers. At last, he was patched up—almost literally—by a doctor from a mission at Marangu, sent for by runner. Things didn't look very good concerning the wounds that had not been disinfected, but in three months Kittenberger was again ambulatory.

Seven years later, Kittenberger's servant Najsebwa was badly mauled by a lioness that reared up on her hind legs and nearly tore the black's shoulder off with a paw blow. On this occasion, it's worth mentioning, Kittenberger was carrying a Mannlicher-Schoenauer rifle of 8-mm and had another problem. This is not a condemnation by any means of modern European ammo, but a bullet became stuck in the barrel while he was busy shooting quite a reasonable stack of *Simbas*. To quote him, "It was a common occurrence with Austrian cartridges for a bullet to be separated from the case and get stuck in the bore." This was the primary reason that Walter Bell, lord of the .256 on elephants, gave up the caliber. He also used early Austrian ammo, and recorded quite a few head separations with the stuff.

It has often been commented that the ripping, tearing, and biting done by a lion are at the time of the mauling painless. The thesis probably originated with David Livingstone, who was half-digested by a *Simba* in the Bechuanaland area when his altruistic backside became intimately involved with a wounded lion showing no sense of community commitment. I don't want to beat a dead lion, but the reports vary widely on the pain experienced when coming out second best with *Simba*, as reported by those who have done the deed. Livingstone claimed that there was no discomfort until later, as have many other recipients of lionization. Yet all people are not of the same opinion. Paul Nielssen, who had his leg broken and several meatloafs removed by a wounded lion, as reported in *Death in the Long Grass*, very definitely felt pain. Or, how about agony? Kittenberger would have as soon done a matinee with the Spanish Inquisition. So too another half-dozen unlucky or clumsy lion victims of my acquaintance. One man, severely chewed up by a lion, described each bite as feeling as if nine-inch nails were being pounded through his flesh. Apparently, the sensation of pain depends upon individual circumstances that may, for reasons unknown at least to this scribe, be either severe or nonexistent. I have been reasonably badly hurt on three instances; one was excruciating and the other two as impersonal as if seen on TV.

Certainly, there is a shock value, both physical and psychological, to the initial impact of confrontation with something as imposing as a lion. As any combat veteran will tell you, the chemicals released by the brain under circumstances of terminal stress frequently numb the normal sensation of pain, which is meant to tell you that you're doing something wrong. Apparently, the same thing commonly applies when being given the once-over by a lion or other biting machine.

There's a wide divergence of opinion as to the durability of the lion, which, except for the leopard, is the smallest and most lightly boned of the Big Five. Not that the average, politically uncommitted, garden-variety lion wouldn't make nearly two of the meanest linebackers in the National Football League were you to grant the gentlemen a fistful of switchblades and a bear trap for a mouth each; a lion is still one hell of a package of perdition. Sure, the Cape buff will take a lot more punishment, as will the rhino and the elephant. But don't ever forget that in the relative scheme of things lions *eat* Cape buffalo!

Somebody who should have known better wrote in happier times that a lion was as easy to kill as a duiker, the 25-pound antelope of the *miombo*. Hell, so is an elephant, if you hit him right the first time. Even though lions don't have the massive muscles and bullet-deflecting bones of the real heavies, they can still hang on to their mortal coils for some impressive time periods before requiring a fresh pressing.

I especially remember one very big lion, not all that much in the hairdo department but a tremendous animal, who was in company with another, back in Rhodesia. The pair of lions flushed in front of me and my clients like great tawny quail, racing off through grass that was twelve feet high and even more lion-colored than they were. "Bust that (expletive and euphemism deleted) on the left!" I shouted in stentorian style as soon as I saw which was the bigger.

The client did, delivering an unfortunate although under the circumstances still very good shot that turned out to be a freak. The bullet from his .375—it *might* have been a .458—caught the *Silwane,* as lions are dubbed in Sindebele, as he headed directly away, and with the unveering slash of a Heidelberg dueling sword sliced the cat completely through the skin of the center of the back, the bullet lodging in the neck. If you had stretched that hide in a frame and swung at the center with a newly honed saber, you wouldn't have done a better—or worse—job. The lion reared up like a bronco with a mixed salad of *cholla* under his saddle, giving me the chance to stick him with a 300-grain Winchester Silvertip pretty well between the shoulders as he went through his rampant phase. To my surprise and growing consternation, he didn't drop cold but flickered off into the vegetable heartburn of amber angina, which swallowed him up like a virgin at the crap tables. That he was delighted with the arrangement was apparent from the growls of unquestionable invitation that he issued at regular intervals. Jesus, but that was one mad lion!

Although I was of course just dying to run into the grass and finish him with my knife or perhaps a vertical buttstroke, I was somehow dissuaded by my clients. Very convincing people. The reminder that I hadn't settled my bar bill back at the Lodge instilled the sense of social responsibility necessary to keep me out of the grass. After all, if I welched on that tab, half the economy of Matabeleland would have collapsed! After a suitable display of temperament, I relented on my chance for a fifth cluster to my Victoria Cross and retired to consider my options.

What you do not want is hand-to-paw combat with even friendly lions. I have been told by those who know me that, on a one-to-one, they would bet on a stale length of baloney even if I were armed with a chain saw. What they don't realize is that I am a responsible person. The unwitting might even mentally mouth the word "coward." I prefer "prudent." My lawyer has a large family. How could he manage without me? My accountant would commit *seppuku* without my quarterly stipends. The bank would surely curl its financial toes without their charges in overdraft penalties. I have a responsibility to society. I will sit down. I will smoke a cigarette, one hundred millimeters at least, and wonder why I don't smoke double Coronas or calabash pipes while waiting for wounded lions to cash in.

I do not like wounded lions. They have advanced tendencies to bite. Not that they scare me, you understand, it's just that I have a tremendous ingrained respect for wildlife. Still, from the sound of it, this is a clear case of noncooperation. The thing in the grass is continuing to suggest that I up and play Daniel, and by the look of the sun, dropping like a redhot cannonball into deep water, I guess I'd better do just that.

I don't think I'm all that sentimental, but I sure do miss that Land Rover, parked miles away, with its nice, secure raised platform on which I would have been able to stand while one of my swarthy stalwarts drove it into the crud until I could see *Nkosi Silwane* through that dozen feet of grass height and give him a nice, neat sendoff. At least there's no question where he is; he's just about as hard to locate as a Dixieland band, given the sounds he's making. I snuff the cigarette just as Ronald Colman would have done it, snicker open the bolt of the old Winchester for the gleam of worn brass, unscrew the tip-off scope, try to think of at least one passing reason why I should be elsewhere, and fail. In I go.

Edging through the grass is rather like going up the down escalator at rush hour when there's a fire at the top. It would be quieter to dance *fandango* on month-old soda crackers. Visibility is four and one-quarter inches past your nifty new yellow-lens Bausch and Lomb shooting glasses, although you somehow doubt that the designers had this in mind. Yonder feline is still being cooperative, though, and by his sound not moving. Maybe he's anchored! Wouldn't that be Jim Dandy! Neat! Let's hear it for the Boy Legend!

He is not broken down, as you notice by a rattling nothing short of a cane manufacturers' convention. He is muttering some very ugly things as he swishes the tops of the stems just as cheerleaders flick their pom-poms, and he is not going away. You know you're not going anywhere unless in a plastic bag, so you kneel and face the racing rustle of death. No running now. You remain firm and shoot. Maybe you live, maybe you die. What the hell. You do your best. Boy, but *do* you.

The first shot goes off just as he's a beige wraith at the edge of vision, the black of the sights lined up right where they should be. Somehow, you know there's a blast and an unfelt recoil; you know it's a solid hit, too. The boil of amber smoke that's trying to kill you swirls, flips. A roar of pain and anger literally shakes the thumb-thick stalks, but it's back on its feet, a reddish cast to the mouth, the eyes as clear and sharp as a couple of your childhood marbles held in your hand. The .375 booms unheard again and you can actually, no-fooling, *see* the bullet as it flickers through a sword of sun to disappear into the lion's chest. As scared as you are, it's marvelous. You can *see* the little flirt of fur as it blows from beneath the chin, the individual hairs drifting to be lost forever, melding with the anonymous tawny fawn of the dead grass below.

The lion has hit some invisible wire that jerks him up short. It's not really bullet impact as much as his own brakes. He stiffens, goes up on tiptoe, and then pitches forward. The momentum he tries to stop overcomes his resistance, and he turns completely over, landing spraddle-legged in a limp pose of death that cannot be a lie. You always know death; the open eye, the bitten-through tongue, the tiny quivers of muscular reaction. But you're a cynic. You shoot him again. They can always sew up the extra hole in Denver or San Antonio. Better his than yours.

The biggest mistake the inexperienced make in trying to stop charging lions is firing too high. I long ago made the decision that, since there was absolutely no point in running, I would get as low as possible and shoot at the level on which the cat was approaching. Lions aren't all that tall and the raking effect of the bullet is what counts: The more organs it puts holes in, the less likely you are to end up in a "This Happened to My Late Friend" sort of story in one of the hunting magazines. Bell swore by solids for lions, and many other pros will opt for them despite what the cartridge boxes may say. I've always wondered who writes the stuff on ammo boxes, anyway. Somehow I suspect that they have not shot very many rhinos or stood up to carloads of lion charges.

When a lion charges, he is not devious. He comes

straight for you. You don't need a George Grey performance with a light slug turning fink on you on the rocky, rugged chest muscles, so I think there is a case for the solid. If you stay low and place a reasonable caliber in his upper chest, it may just give him an optional arsehole, a creation he will be highly unlikely to have any future opportunities to utilize.

It's the deceptive speed of a motivated lion that leads to shooting too high, a bullet meant for the chest often ending up somewhere above the hips or even in a clean miss behind the cat. Hold on the bottom of the chest and count on the microseconds it takes the firing pin to fall, the primer to detonate the power, the power to burn, and the bullet to whisk its spiral line out of the bore, cross the distance, and catch the tabby a couple of yards closer to you than it was when you eased off the trigger. As I've said, lions aren't all that hard to kill, but I once had to shoot a crippled one three times with a .375 through the chest before he waved a mortal white flag. It was embarrassing as hell, but the bullets were going where they were supposed to; he just hadn't gotten the script right.

I don't think many professional hunters would argue that the best all-round shot on a lion is the shoulder or chest shot. From a side angle, I'd prefer a heavily jacketed soft-point such as a Silvertip or Remington Core-Lokt, although I would have no compunction about using a solid bullet on an extended basis for the added value of bone breaking. We've already discussed the frontal shot, but it could save your life one of these days to be advised not to shoot at the head. There's nothing worth damaging above a lion's eyes as he jumps out of the grass facing you, and many's the slug that has caromed off the almost zero-degree slope of the skull as a lion looks at you. Stick him in the chest and continue to do so as long as you can see him.

Of course, what makes lion hunting, uh, er, interesting, is that there's always the risk that one will catch up with your neatly tailored butt. Provided he doesn't bite your head off as some sort of warm-up exercise, the best I can tell you as a man whose experience has happily been limited to the testimonies of surviving pals and eyewitness accounts of the last moments of late friends is that you had better start feeding him arms and legs, as slowly as possible so you don't run out but with sufficient perseverance that he doesn't get a chance to bite you in the head or chest. They can do wonderful things with really chewed up limbs these days, which doesn't sound like much of an ad for lion hunting but is something to consider. You may not win any more frisbee championships or take up brain surgery for fun and profit, but you'll at least live. Of course, you may not, but it's still a happy thought to bear in mind.

One of the more fascinating aspects of presumably emergent Western society is that of the "back-to-nature" syndrome that has become so commercially popular and profitable from the United States to Australia and Europe. Well, with most of us up to our collective navels in our own cultural flotsam and jetsam, it's understandable that we may still yearn for the benign roar of a caged lion or the throttled trumpet of a hostage elephant. I'm no sociologist, but the fact remains that "Lion Parks" are the rage wherever there's space to locate one. After all, not many folks have the airfare from Seattle to Nairobi to hear what is nearly the real thing, and there's still something subliminal in our souls that craves the proximity of predators. Perhaps

229

the bloody movies we watch are offshoots of this, but that's a story for another book.

As John Hunter observed, the nature of game has changed, and lions are no exception. Yet, where some species practically evaporate at the merest smell of man, the modern game park lion has become far, far more dangerous because he's lost his ancestral fear of people. In fact, to some extent he associates humans with food in a variety of ways. You don't need a Doctorate in Zoology to figure out that this isn't good news.

I recently saw something in the Gulf of Mexico town of Naples, Florida, that really brought that fact home. There's a very attractive tourist magnet called Jungle Larry and Safari Jane's African Safari. It's a well-run, really interesting wild animal display that has collected a few awards for cleanliness and imagination as well as having been the place where the famous tiglons were bred. With a tiger father and a lioness mother, they're not unique but nearly so. That one of the tiglons badly injured a child some years ago was certainly no fault of the Jungle Larry operation, which has everything but minefields to keep their clients out of harm's way, but then there are some people who just don't believe in signs and ranks of barbed wire. These are the same people whose genetic traits the Yellowstone Park and Glacier Park bears have tried to eliminate through most active natural selection; with some admirable success, I might add. Unfortunately, we just don't have enough bears to go around and from time to time lions are obliged to fill in.

The incident I witnessed had no fatal consequences, but it was none the less fascinating to watch.

There was a small family group of people, Mom, Dad, and a child of about three. I was standing next to the hurricane fence that I really suspect protects the lions more than the people, or at least I thought so at the time. There was a very hirsute male *Simba* lying tangled in a well-assorted pile of dozing lady lions and cubs when I saw a great amber eye open and take in the apparent lunch wandering by about thirty yards away across the enclosure. Instantly, the lion was wide awake, flattened on the worn grass, with eyes locked onto the child like a heat-seeking missile. I have no idea what it was about the kid; maybe the old boy was just hungry or perhaps there was something special about the way the child toddled along. With my mouth hanging open, I watched that big cat slither forward about ten yards, pause, and then come in a flat-out charge.

There were maybe a dozen people near the lion fence, and if whoever cleans out the elephant enclosure thinks he has a big job, the man who sweeps up outside the lion paddock must have been astonished when next he wandered by with his broom and dustpan. It was a classic attack rush, the tail high and rigid, the mouth half-open, a chilling series of grunts bludgeoning the air. Women screamed and men shouted. I just sort of stood there in purest amazement. The lion—maybe he was newly captured?—hit that fence hard enough to make the steel support posts ring, while the flexible hurricane wire threw him back several feet like a topspin tennis serve. He got up, looked at the wire and the kid, muttered something in four-letter lionese, and went back to the pile of pussies. Do you want to tell me he wouldn't have eaten that kid if he could have caught him? You'd better start early if you want to convince me otherwise. I was *there*.

Some people aren't lucky enough to be behind steel

fences. How about this report from the Associated Press on July 24, 1982, less than a month back as I write this. . . .

LIONS KILL VISITOR FOR PETTING CUB

Stockholm, Sweden, July 24, 1982—A man who stepped out of his car today to pet a lion cub in an animal park was killed by three lions, police said.

The man, identified only as a 42-year-old Stockholmer, was visiting the Kolmarden Zoo 150 kilometers south of Stockholm. After entering the gates to the lions' section, the man detoured from the visitors route and stopped the car. He opened the door and stepped out to touch a lion cub.

"A lioness came forward, knocked him to the ground and used its jaws to rip his throat," witnesses said.

Two male lions then attacked the man and started to drag him away.

The badly mauled man died minutes after wardens had scared the lions away and driven off with him.

Well, talk about an advanced death wish. . . .

It's odd how frequently lions figure in coincidences. The very same day that the Disneyized Stockholmer was getting torn apart by lions in Sweden, practically on the other side of the earth a nearly identical episode was in progress in Perth, Australia. Both the following reports, the first from *The Miami Herald* and the second from the Natal *Mercury* of Durban, South Africa, pretty clearly illustrate my contention that lions are far more dangerous after association with man than before.

MAN EATEN BY LIONS AFTER IGNORING SIGNS

Perth, West Australia, July 24, 1982—A man who failed to heed warning signs and got out of his car in a wildlife park was mauled to death Saturday by 15 hungry lions, police said.

Peter Zakovic, 42, of Perth, was ripped apart by the lions, who had been waiting for their mid-morning feeding at Wanneroo Safari Park, north of Perth. Officials said Zakovic had walked up to the lions.

Park officials were summoned when a distraught woman and her two children saw frenzied lions fighting over what turned out to be the man's body. Park manager Steve Crane fired blank shells to scare off the lions and recover the body.

LIONS RIP APART AUSTRALIAN DANIEL

Sydney, Australia, July 24, 1982—A religious fanatic who tried to imitate the biblical Daniel walked into a lion enclosure at the weekend—and was torn apart by 15 adult lions.

The man, in his early 40's and wearing a number of crucifixes and religious medallions, got out of his car in Wanneroo Safari Park north of Perth.

He locked the car, then walked about 50 meters to where the lions were feeding.

He started patting them, but they jumped on him, threw him to the ground and began to tear him apart.

Terrified visitors called the manager.

He drove into the enclosure and fired a shotgun to frighten off the lions, but they refused to leave their prey.

Eventually he had to charge at them in his car to force them away.

The man, whose identity has not yet been revealed, was dead when an ambulance arrived.

By far the more dangerous artificial environment in which to encounter a lion under modern tourist conditions is that of an African game park or reserve, excepting, of course, in circumstances of hunting. Although "lion parks" outside of Africa are usually extremely careful about sealing car doors and otherwise discouraging "modern Daniels," even to the extent of not permitting convertibles with cloth tops, we've seen that not a hell of a lot has changed between man the prey and lion the carnivore.

Man-eaters are among the most fascinating of animals, and I just can't resist telling you about a recent adventure of a black African game warden in the area of Mala Mala, a private game reserve in South Africa near the Kruger Park in the Transvaal.

He is Elfas Mbungla, a Shangaan tribesman married to a woman named Vina. It was March of 1981 and Elfas had been on leave with his twenty-three-year-old wife but decided to return to work a day early. Walking through the bush, they hoofed it back to within five miles of the Mala Mala reserve before blackness began to fall, stopping at a hut on the Sand River to spend the night. It was a standard thatched affair but had a bed and mattress, an odd length of metal pipe, a few empty soft-drink bottles, and a working kerosene lamp with a nearly full reservoir. A "trail hut" for the use of the wardens, it was comfortable enough, and Vina went out to collect firewood while the thirty-five-year-old Elfas, a slender, lightly built man, puttered around waiting for Vina to return.

234

His wife's shriek broke his thoughts. A lioness, old, decrepit, and desperate, had caught the woman and lay atop her, having severely bitten her thighs and buttocks. Vina never knew where the lioness had come from but managed to get an arm up to protect her head, an arm that the starving lioness badly crushed between her rotting and broken teeth. She was the rare but classic man-eater, too savage with starvation and injury to fear attacking man.

Elfas Mbungla was out of the half-door in one movement, his hand clutching the first weapon that came within reach. It was a well-worn broom. Running toward the sound of Vina's screams, he came on the twilight scene and smacked the lioness over the back until the broom handle splintered. Refusing to leave the wounded woman, the lioness ignored him but for furious snarls. In a growing panic, Elfas dashed back to the hut and loaded up with empty bottles, rocks, and anything else he could find to throw. Incredibly, the lioness melted off into the dark bush. Dragging the mauled Vina, Elfas managed to get back into the hut and slam the flimsy door.

Elfas had a hard look in the low light at Vina's wounds, which were severe but not fatal. As he tried to figure out what to do, a low rumble came from the now open door. The lioness stood there, her mouth open, having returned to collect her meal.

Mbungla lunged for the piece of pipe and swung it as hard as he could at the lioness' head. He missed. To his horror, the door collapsed under the impact of the pipe. With growing terror, he heard his wife ask through her pain if she was going to die. "I will save you," answered Elfas, but one wonders if he believed it at the time.

Thinking in overdrive, Elfas recalled the kerosene

lamp and the heavy overcoat he wore against the chill of the autumn March evening. Ripping the coat into strips, he soaked them in kerosene—locally called paraffin—lit them, and flipped them at the threatening lioness. Snarling, the big cat withdrew for a few moments.

Having inadvertently smashed the door with the pipe, Elfas snatched the mattress off the bed and tried to jam the opening with it. All was quiet outside as he stuffed a pair of pillows into the windows, sealing them with scraps left over from the coat. Elfas didn't know it as he mixed some salt into water to treat his wife's wounds, but fifteen hours would pass before the nightmare of the man-eater would be over.

A rasping snarl and pawstroke shocked him upright over the moaning body of Vina as the remains of the coat were torn from the windowframe. So starving was the lioness that she actually ate the green-beige overcoat, buttons and all. Sure that his number was up, Elfas let his mind race over how to save his wife. Although the hut didn't have a high roof, Elfas tore a hole in the thatch and shoved his wife through it. Vina was too badly injured to hang in place by herself, so Elfas used his belt to secure her to the outer rafters, expecting to die fighting the lioness below.

The hours crawled by, blackness tinted with the groans and snarls of the lioness as she kept returning. In one of her assaults, she ate kapok-filled pillows that had been stuffed into a window. Every few minutes, the rasp of claws on dry grass paralyzed the couple, but Elfas began to realize that the large overhang of the thatch roof offered insufficient support for the lioness, so she could not reach them, shivering under the starlight.

Dawn broke as a mango tint in the east. There was

no sight or sign of the lioness, but Elfas and his wife slipped from the roof and crossed the river to prevent the cat from following them up. By this time, Elfas was completely mute, his voice gone from shouting at the lioness all night long.

It was six months before woodcutters found the desiccated body of the lioness, well processed by hyenas and vultures, apparently starved to death by her failure to kill and eat one or both of the Mbunglas. The morning after the attack, the spoor of the lioness had been wiped away by a sudden rain, but the tattered remains of the cat indicated that she had died shortly after the attack on the couple. Fluffy kapok from the eaten pillows and shreds of Elfas' coat were littered near the bones, some particles windblown into the thornbushes. The lioness, from the informal postmortem, had been so desperate that she had eaten a porcupine. The teeth of the sun-whitened skull were broken, worn, and diseased, and only one claw was found near the scavenger-ravaged carcass. It was mounted in silver and presented to Elfas Mbungla by—who else—Gary Player. Elfas Mbungla is now the head warden of a large section of the Mala Mala Reserve.

I find it nostalgic to sign off a chapter on lions, particularly as they have been such a major factor in my life—and several times of equal consideration in what then seemed to be my impending death. Still, when the fire is low, and the razor blade of moon just a flicker, there's always the cry of the Old Africa, the call that so clearly says that man will never be completely dominant over the ancient but nubile black body of the lady who really controls my heart. The KiSwahili speakers understand the lion's long *UUUUnnnHHHH, Uhhh, Uhhh, Uhhh,* best, I think, interpreting the hollow, echoing challenge of *Simba* that rolls across the liquid darkness of rivers and the muted greenish dun of plain from incredible miles as follows:

"Hi inchi ya nani?" translate the tribesmen with the secret suppression of a shudder. "Whose land is this?"

"Yangu, yangu, yangu."

"Mine, mine, mine."

Believe it, Charlie.